HYDRO DIPLOMACY

SHARING WATER ACROSS BORDERS

Editor

Ganesh Pangare

IUCN

ECOSYSTEMS FOR LIFE
A BANGLADESH-INDIA INITIATIVE

BRIDGE

AF
ACADEMIC FOUNDATION

Credits

Published by: Academic Foundation, 4772/23, Bharat Ram Road, 23 Ansari Road, Daryaganj, New Delhi - 110 002.

Citation: Pangare Ganesh, editor (2014) Hydro-Diplomacy : Sharing Water Across Borders, New Delhi, India: Academic Foundation, 154 pp

Concept: Ambassador Shiv Mukherjee, Ambassador C M Shafi Sami and Ganesh Pangare

Coordination: Lalita Rammont, Bushra Nishat and Lisa Binti Idris

Project Team: Archana Chatterjee, Mohammad Shahad Mahabub Chowdhury, Brian Furze, Lisa Binti Idris, Sushmita Mandal, Bushra Nishat, Ganesh Pangare, AJM Zobaidur Rahman Soeb and Lalita Rammont.

Cover Design and Layout: Rustam Vania

Cartoons: Rustam Vania

Financed by: The Minister for Foreign Trade and Development Cooperation, the Netherlands and IUCN

Available from:

IUCN Asia Regional Office
63 Sukhumvit Soi 39
Sukhumvit Road, Wattana
Bangkok 10110, Thailand
Tel: +662 662 4029
Fax: +662 662 4387

IUCN Bangladesh Country Office
House 16, Road 2/3, Banani,
Dhaka 1213, Bangladesh
Tel: +8802 9890423, Fax: +8802 9892854
www.iucn.org/bangladesh

IUCN India Country Office
B 88, Neeti Bagh, New Delhi - 110049, INDIA
Tel/Fax: +91 11 4605 2583, 26527742
www.iucn.org/india

HYDRO DIPLOMACY

SHARING WATER ACROSS BORDERS

Content and Contributors

Abbreviations and Acronyms

ADB	- Asian Development Bank
ADR	- Alternative Dispute Resolution
APWF	- Asia Pacific Water Forum
AWDO	- Asian Water Development Outlook
CEPAL	- La Comisión Económica para América Latina
EIA	- Environmental Impact Assessment
EU	- European Union
GDP	- Gross Domestic Product
GEF	- Global Environment Facility
GS/OAS	- General Secretariat of the Organization of American States
GWP	- Global Water Partnership
ICWC	- Interstate Commission for Water Coordination in Central Asia
IHP	- International Hydrological Programme
ISARM	- Internationally Shared Aquifer Resources Management
IUCN	- International Union for Conservation of Nature
IWRM	- Integrated Water Resources Management
JRC	- Joint River Commission
MDG	- Millennium Development Goals
MRC	- Mekong River Commission
MSIOA	- Multi-Sector Investment Opportunities Analysis
OAS	- Organization of American States
OMVS	- Organisation pour la Mise en Valeur du Fleuve Sénégal
PCCP	- Potential Conflict to Cooperation Potential
PIDS	- Inter American Program on Sustainable Development
RBO	- River Basin Organization
SIWI	- Stockholm International Water Institute
UN	- United Nations
UNDP	- United Nations Development Programmme
UNECE	- United Nations Economic Commission for Europe
UNEP	- United Nations Environment Programme
UNESCO	- United Nations Educational Scientific and Cultural Organization
UNESCO-IHP	- UNESCO's International Hydrological Programme
UNICEF	- United Nations International Children's Emergency Fund
US-CAFTA	- United States – Central America Free Trade Agreement

Acknowledgements

This monograph has been conceptualised and written by IUCN Water Programme, Asia Regional Office, Bangkok with authors from across the world. IUCN acknowledges and thanks all of the authors for sharing their experience, thoughts and ideas, without which this publication would not have been possible

Our sincere thanks goes to Ambassadors' Shiv Shankar Mukherjee and C.M. Shafi Sami, Project Advisory Committee (PAC) members of the Ecosystem for Life: A Bangladesh India Initiative, who were instrumental in conceptualising the monograph and supporting the process of putting it together. We would also like to express our thanks to all the members of the PAC for their invaluable support.

The monograph is a follow up of the International Conference on Hydro-diplomacy: A Tool for Sharing Water across Borders, held in Chiang Rai, Thailand on 31 October 2012. It is important to thank all the 120 participants, especially the speakers and presenters. A very special thanks to H.E. Preecha Rengsomboonsuk, Minister of the Ministry of Natural Resources and Environment of the Kingdom of Thailand for inaugurating the workshop. Also to H.E. Gopalkrishna Gandhi, Former Governor of West Bengal, India, who despite his very busy schedule came and delivered the special address. And thanks to Prof Torkil Jønch Clausen a long time friend and advisor to IUCN for giving the keynote address at the workshop. Thanks to Shri Subrata Mukherjee, Hon'ble Cabinet Minister, Department of Public Health Engineering, Panchayat and Rural Development, Government of West Bengal, India and to Jerry Delli Prescoli who facilitated the workshop. And to Khaled Abu–Zeid, Yum Kyungtaek, Teferra Beyene, Gordon Johnson, Hans Guttman, and Chirs Morger.

To Aban Marker Kabraji, Regional Director, IUCN Asia Regional Office (ARO) for her constant support and encouragement to this initiative and to T.P. Singh, Deputy Regional Director Programmes, IUCN, ARO. Mark Smith, Alejandro Iza, Rocio Cordoba, Michael Dougherty, Claire Warmenbol, Ishtiaq Uddin Ahmad, Meenakshi Datta Ghosh, P.R. Sinha, Latsamay Sylavong, Rosa Mary Saengsanthitham, Robert Mather, Kanokphorn Pudpa, Kulkanya Hiranyasthiti, Dararat Weerapong, Tawatchai Rattanasorn, Tanyathon Phetmanee, Jake Brunner, Kong Kimsreng, Nguyen Duc Tu, Monica Zavagli, Mario Aguirre, Raphael Glemet of IUCN who have been a constant support to the Water Programme. Finally, to all our colleagues at the Asia Regional Office and country offices in the region.

To Ian Makin, Indira Chakravarty, Léna Salamé, Anada Tiega, Arzu Rana Deuba, Meena Gupta, Yoonjin Kim, who were constantly around when support, help and advice was needed.

To Rustam Vania for his brilliant cartoons and Sanu Kapila and Sona Kapila from Academic Foundation for their constant support and encouragement, and for bringing this book out under a very tight deadline. And a special thanks to Lalita Rammont,

Bushra Nishat, Lisa Binti Idris Sushmita Mandal and Brian Furze for help in the production of this monograph.

Above all, we are grateful to: Minister for Foreign Trade and Development Cooperation, the Netherlands and the Embassy of the Kingdom of the Netherlands, Dhaka for their constant encouragement and support, specifically to Carel de Groot, Michiel Slotema, A.T.M. Khaleduzzaman and Ambassador Gerben de Jong. To the Ministry of Foreign Affairs of Finland and Antti Inkinen and Srin Boonyoung and to the Swiss Agency for Development Cooperation and Johan Gely. We sincerely thank these development partners for their support and trust to IUCN.

Preface

Shiv Mukherjee

IT IS a common place comment, for some years now, to say that the 20th century was about oil, and the 21st century is about water. The U.N. has declared 2013 as the 'International Year of Water Cooperation'. What impact this will have on the nations of planet Earth is another matter, but it may be in order to depart from cynicism and accept that the world body's underlining of the fundamental issues relating to water management is to be welcomed.

It is to IUCN's credit that it focused on one important aspect of the multiple problems relating to water and river issues, which is the question of trans-boundary river flows, between neighbouring nations, and even between states in a nation with a federal structure.

A U.N. report points out that water disputes have almost never led to war. The only recorded 'water war' was between the city states of Lagash and Umma, 4500 years ago. Indeed, nations have used, according to the report, sharing of waters as a "neutralising" factor in conflict situations. An example given is the Indus Water Treaty between India and Pakistan; neighbours which have gone to war four times, yet keeping the sanctity of the Treaty intact. However the same report points out that, 30 nations of the world will be "water scarce" by 2025, leading to potential conflicts, of which 18 are in West Asia and North Africa, making this the "hot-spot" of looming conflicts over water.

The absence of "war" is not really the absence of "conflict". Water management issues, sharing of river waters, mutual suspicions and insecurities in upper and lower riparian countries, ever increasing demands caused by increasing populations, climate change, deforestation and resulting floods and soil erosion—all these lead to a vitiated atmosphere between neighbouring nations, that can and do bedevil relations at every level, inevitably affecting the daily lives of people on both sides.

Most importantly, any solution must be acceptable at all levels, in all the countries involved, especially at the popular level, the level of the people. Therefore the need for political will, as in all matters of state, is to seek not the ideal solution, but the best possible under the circumstances. Unfortunately, this most important factor is usually the most elusive. It is naïve to exhort governments to keep politics out of technical matters and leave it to professional and experts. At the end of the day, everything depends on political expediency, political perceptions, and political will.

Is it time to take this idea forward? Again, how do we encourage and bring to fruition the political will to do this? One can only hope that this is a reminder to all stakeholders that time is running out, and corrective action is needed now, for tomorrow may well be too late.

HYDRO ETHICS
HYDRO PHILOSOPHY
HYDRO CALLOUSNESS
HYDRO INTELLIGENCE
HYDRO COMMON SENSE
HYDRO RIGHTS
HYDRO POLITICS
HYDRO SOCIOLOGY
HYDRO COMPETITION
HYDRO SOLIDARITY
HYDRO DIPLOMACY
HYDRO PERSUASION
HYDRO LOGIC

SHARING WATER ACROSS BORDERS

Perspectives on Hydro-Diplomacy

Ganesh Pangare and Bushra Nishat

HYDRO-DIPLOMACY is a dynamic process and works under the premise that shared benefits of water cooperation will result in mutually acceptable benefits for riparian states. Negotiations over shared waters hinge on economics, legal frameworks, international law, international relations, geopolitics and hydrology. Cooperation for water management is a long-term social, political and diplomatic effort and needs to be revisited and adapted according to the prevailing situation. Hydro-diplomacy could increasingly play an important role in strengthening and securing international relations and regional stability provided that it demonstrates concrete results on the ground; results for water, food and energy security, for a green economy, for healthy ecosystems and climate resilience, for people's health and well being and equity.

An international conference organised by IUCN on *Hydro-diplomacy: A Tool for Sharing Water Across Borders* was held on 31 October 2012. This conference brought together over 120 diplomats, political scientists, economists, water resource professionals and related experts to discuss and deliberate on the complexities of hydro-diplomacy. This monograph integrates learning from these discussions and is a compilation of thoughts, ideas, and reflections on hydro-diplomacy from different parts of the world. It is an attempt to put together perspectives from a wide range of stakeholders on their views and understanding about what hydro-diplomacy entails.

Across the globe, investments in infrastructure development such as roads, embankments, barrages, dams, diversions, irrigation schemes and power facilities, while bringing some visible benefits at the local and national level, are also creating multiple burdens and risks to the river and millions of people who are dependant for their lives and livelihoods on the rivers, associated wetlands and aquatic resources. In the case of international rivers, these risks and burdens are made more complex by sovereignty implications and geopolitical dimensions. Integrated water resources management (IWRM), a well-established and widely accepted concept, advocates the concept of the basin as the unit of planning and management so as to address cross-sectoral and multi-dimensional stakeholder interests. In order to make such planning and management possible, there would have to be cooperation between sectors, between states in federal governments, between countries and governments. Hydro-diplomacy could help countries and governments to move towards a perspective of shared opportunities for positive regional benefits, while keeping in mind national and local needs and interests. Hydro-diplomacy tries to harmonise water policies and standards and brings into focus issues at different levels and across sectors, encompassing not only technical but also social and economic implications.

Agreements or treaties between riparian countries are mostly bilateral and may or may not have a holistic approach to river management. The conventional approach to hydro-diplomacy has been mostly focussed on negotiations on formulating a formal agreement or 'treaty' between two governments. The details of this agreement are usually prescribed by diplomats, government delegates and bureaucrats based on international conventions and standards. According to IUCN (2013), this approach presumes hydro-diplomacy takes place under the authority of sovereign governments. While formal agreements at the official level are absolutely necessary, this approach often disregards that water resources is managed at multiple scales, thus for these agreements to work on the ground and to be acceptable at the national or country level, involvement of water users at different levels including local communities are also essential. A wide spectrum of formal and informal agreements, concentrating on concrete actions and sustainable solutions based on local priorities need to be in place. This means an all-inclusive approach with participation and involvement of a broad range of stakeholders including local communities, local governments, technical agencies, economic and private sectors. These agreements would then become the practical building blocks that augment and improve the potential for national governments to reach high-level agreements encouraging an operational roadmap for improvement in water governance towards sustainable development at the basin level (IUCN, 2013). Hydro-diplomacy approaches have the potential to play a facilitating and bridge-building role to support and enable these agreements to be put in place at different levels and between governments. Hydro-diplomacy starts with national interests, and needs to be embedded in effective processes from the initial dialogue to being able to progress all the way to a constructive and enforceable agreement and its joint implementation at national and regional levels between riparian interests.

Water cooperation is an issue that has received a great deal of attention and focus from development aid agencies. With growing environmental concerns and strong disagreement about water infrastructures, the international community is looking at facilitating trust building processes, focusing not only on knowledge management, thematic studies, environmental monitoring but also on ensuring soft skills towards improving political sensitivity and negotiation. There is greater affirmation of the importance of transparency and participation in the process, integrating a gender perspective and participation of civil society and local communities in water diplomacy. The international communities are giving greater emphasis on stronger investment cooperation at the basin scale. Some of our authors have used the term 'cooperative investment to achieve a common goal' in describing this.

The common goal should not be focused only on infrastructure development, but also on environmental conservation, information and monitoring systems, legal frameworks, and accompanying institutions.

How does hydro-diplomacy work? How can it become an effective tool? How can hydro-diplomacy be put into practice? The answers lie in addressing three key challenges:

a) building consensus,
b) building institutions for hydro-diplomacy; and
c) identifying and catalysing the processes necessary to mobilise hydro-diplomacy.

It is important to keep in mind that consensus building in hydro-diplomacy starts with national interests, including economic development, security, and concerns and needs of the local population. Consensus building then requires trust and political will, platforms for dialogue and transparency, knowledge and information, capacity and tools for integration of competing demands and for identifying mutual benefits. Institutions for hydro-diplomacy include "truly" representative river basin organisations (RBOs) that involve different stakeholders. RBOs need to work alongside other regional platforms across sectors and with the drivers of change in different rivers and different basins. Agreements will work on the ground only if they involve water users and have their support and take into account local politics.

In order to catalyse and mobilise hydro-diplomacy, it is necessary to have in place processes in national agendas and in international dialogues, and also processes that support interaction with stakeholders. Education of stakeholders, communication and capacity development, and strengthening of national institutions is required in order to make these processes effective. Platforms and partnerships for dialogue that work across sectors and constituencies, and inform and backstop governments would need to be put in place. Effective governance at the national level, sound policies and laws that align with trans-boundary issues would also need to align with hydro-diplomacy processes. There would need to be a better understanding of the issues that countries and citizens want to solve and what their concerns are. Lastly, it would be necessary to drive the application of the existing international processes related to water.

Hydro-diplomacy stems from the need to negotiate where competing and even conflicting interests towards shared water resources are present. National institutions involved in the management of water in transboundary rivers focus on their own national interests, often with consequences to the riparian needs and interests of the countries with whom they share the water resources. As pressures on water resources continue to increase with the prospect of climate change, population growth and fast developing technologies for water abstraction, water allocation and sharing between transboundary riparian states is likely to create frequent and more intense tensions. In response to this challenging reality, hydro-diplomacy could prove to be a crucial tool in ensuring that shared water resources are managed efficiently, sustainably and equitably.

References

International Union for Conservation of Nature IUCN, (2013). Water Diplomacy and Governance in Transboundary Hot Spots (BRIDGE) 2011-2012. Swiss Development Cooperation Grant. End of Phase Report: February 1, 2011 – March 31, 2013.

HYDRODIPLOMACY
ARE YOU SURE?

HYDRO ETHICS
HYDRO PHILOSOPHY
HYDRO CALLOUSNESS
HYDRO INTELLIGENCE
HYDRO COMMON SENSE
HYDRO RIGHTS
HYDRO POLITICS
HYDRO SOCIOLOGY
HYDRO COMPETITION
HYDRO SOLIDARITY
HYDRO DIPLOMACY
HYDRO PERSUASION
HYDRO LOGIC

SHARING WATER ACROSS BORDERS

Hydro-Wisdom must back Hydro-Diplomacy

Gopalkrishna Gandhi

TIME WAS when rivers were rivers and water, water. Rivers defined places, gave human habitations their name.

I come from one of those countries which derive their very name from a river—Sindhu or the Indus.

The doctrine of life—Hinduism—to which the great majority of Indians have for centuries adhered also borrows its name from the same river. And yet only a small sliver of the Indus flows through India today.

Did the great river change its course to make India all but lose its name-giving river? No. We did, we who inhabit what was the India of the Indus.

By 'the Punjab' was meant the land of five rivers. Today there are two Punjabs and neither holds all five rivers.

There was a time when rivers 'held' territories, defining their boundaries, giving their people a certain personality and both land and people, a certain ethos.

The people of the Cauvery delta in India's south had thingness to them. They raised paddy for centuries over three annual cycles. They did more: from the prosperity their white grain brought them, they created and sustained a body of classical music and a tradition of temple architecture and bronze sculpting that remains unsurpassed for its grace and dignity.

Those living in the similarly fecund but much larger Indo-Gangetic Plain also bore a similar stamp. They raised a variety of grains and millets and made the banks of the Ganga and Yamuna host architecture the likes of what had not been seen. The one and only Taj Mahal stands serene beside the Yamuna as a child might along its mother. The Hooghly, as the Ganga gets called at its eastern extremity holds the great Dakshineswar temple near Kolkata in its arms.

Today rivers do not hold us, we hold them. Their waters are not waters. They are electricity—both real as in 'hydel' and metaphorical as in 'thermal' —angry. They electrify those who use them as well as those who feel they should also be using them.

Rivers today have become political entities.

Just as poverty could become a powerful ideology's trigger, and prosperity a no less powerful monopoly's preserve, so have rivers become the subject and the tool for geo-political contestations.

They are flowing arguments, fluid acrimonies. They enrage, infuriate. They can be incendiary.

It would be more accurate, I think, and more fair, to say they have been made to do this. For, with all their mobility, their often torrential energy, their incessant and restless forward movement, rivers are not sentient beings. They owe their physical vigour to nothing other than volume responding to gravity. But such is the enormity of their unwilled physical force, and such the impact of that force on the psychologies and economies of entire populations, that they can be said to be living, pulsating beings.

Men will give their lives for perceived riparian rights.

None will care a fig for riparian duties, obligations, for riparian graces.

'Graces?' one can hear an exclamation. 'Which world are you living in? Rivers are about hard politics, about support-bases, popularity. Rivers are instruments of proxy wars. There is as much room for graces as there would be in battle-trenches during combat'.

And yet, not all that long ago, we did see on the sub-continent of India examples of what may be called a calibrated grace, a measured graciousness, a calculated reposing of faith by both sides. The Indus Waters Treaty between India and Pakistan of 1960, partitioning so to say the Indus river between the western and eastern rivers came after hard negotiations marked by caution as well as risk-taking because the scars of Partition were fresh on both sides and the Kashmir issue loomed large over the talks. This made the Treaty all the more remarkable. The Treaty had its critics at the time and has creative resuscitators of that criticism, with new issues being raised, even today giving Indus water issues to the status of a new 'core issue'.

Land and water are never just about land and water. They touch deep veins of belonging, ownership and attachment. The word 'honour' is never far from any discourse on these two gifts of nature to human proprietorship. We are concerned here about what happens between nations. But it is a commonplace to see murders being committed over land and water. And so counsels of despair are heard about the Indus Treaty. To give up on the Treaty today would be to give in to hard-liners whose interest is not in resolving but reviving disputes. And that would be the highest un-wisdom.

Jihadists as we now know of them did not exist in 1960, but nor was there in vogue then the ingenious device of Track II negotiations preparing the ground for inter-State negotiations. So, if there is a new complication, there is a new process of negotiation now available and in use as well. A new third element has emerged which must be factored in, and that is the new consciousness about the environmental impact of large and large numbers of projects on river systems and, indeed, of climate change.

India and Bangladesh have been in that kind of hydro-discussion over the decades. And it must be said to the credit of both countries that they have tried, often in vain, but never without earnestness, to arrive at solutions.

Where territories were identified by rivers, rivers belong to countries now. But that is an oversimplification. A river may belong to a country but it flows in a specific part or parts of a country and those parts have an affinity with the river amounting to a sense of ownership. And so when India and Bangladesh discuss the rivers that cross into each other's sovereign territories, one has to remember that the state of West Bengal has to have its own perception. India is, so to say, the house where these rivers belong, but West Bengal is their home.

The Ganges Treaty of 1996 saw a fine balancing of this factor, with the then Chief Minister of West Bengal Shri Jyoti Basu playing an important, indeed, crucial part in hydro-diplomacy. At one level the equal sharing of the flows at Farakka so that the quantum available for sharing is not diminished was an engineering matter. At another it was a deeply psychological, social, cultural and political issue. No hydro-agreement can work on the ground unless it has the endorsement and, indeed, the support of the users of water who, in Tamil, are called the ayacutdars. And these users are not to be guided by their own immediate interests. They may be willing to share but only after they have seen to their own needs with a little extra thrown in as well, by way of insurance. How is the river's in-built move from snowmelt to sea, with or without augmentation by rains mid-stream, be explained to riparian along the way as something that has to be shared? Hydro-education at home has to precede hydro-diplomacy if hydro-protocols are not to be scuttled by hydro-politics.

As negotiations between India and Pakistan on the Indus waters, between India and Bangladesh on Teesta and other rivers, between India and China on the Brahmaputra, between India and Nepal on the Kosi and other rivers with reference to flood-prevention must continue, we must realise that hydro-diplomacy is an optimistic expression that seeks to reduce the highly intricate and often fraught process of negotiations to something of a magician's sleight of hand. There can be good solutions, lasting for several years at a stretch, to water related issues but no wishful formulas for solution.

There are far too many stakeholders in water disputes, each stakeholder being assiduously turned into lobby by vested interests who want to, so to say, 'hold' the river in order to hold constituencies, hold support-bases, and thereby, hold on to power. The process of discussing cross-border river water issues therefore requires technological expertise, socio-psychological sensitivity about things like 'honour', local and very fractious angles, counter-lobbying skills and political courage, and then only thereafter the right diplomatic initiative. Without any of the other elements, diplomatic negotiations in themselves cannot hope to succeed. Hydro-diplomacy must be accompanied and in fact preceded by hydro-intelligence, hydro-common-sense and hydro-frankness and, beyond that, by a strong understanding of the political realities that obtain in upper riparian and lower riparian territories and, no less importantly, in mid-riparian transit lands. Hydro-diplomacy has, therefore, to reckon not just with the opposite number in hydro-diplomacy but with the vast and complex hinterland of the hydro-issues in terms of hydro-sociology, hydro-psychology, hydro-politics, hydro-one-upmanship. Indeed, also upper riparian hydro-hubris, mid-riparian hydro-cunning and lower riparian hydro-suspiciousness at all stages of the river's progress. Hydro-diplomacy has to deal with hydro-cleverness, hydro-cunning, hydro-cussedness. It has to cut through these with hydro-logic, hydro-reasoning, hydro-persuasion.

Over all, hydro-diplomacy is hindered by something else as well—hydro-callousness and hydro-complacency among the generality of people not in the direct path of rivers. Far too many of us, who benefit from the fundamentally iniquitous water regime of our times, remain uncaring about the looming water crisis we are going to face.

Water is, let us face it, going to be humanity's crisis number one.

With global warming, population spikes and water-abstraction intensifications, river water and ground water are going to come under unprecedented strain.
But is the world really getting worked up?

The honest answer is no.

Water is the Cinderella of our times. Honest, hard-working, and taken utterly for granted.

The way ground water is plummeting the world over, is unimaginable, unforgivable. How can someone merely because he has the money and the means drill the earth to pull out as much water as he wants?

Sometimes I think a really bad water shock following two or three consecutive years of drought is what the world needs to make it wake up. The problem is that if that were to happen only the already wretched will become more wretchedly hurt.

But I suggest that from this conference we see the beginnings of five initiatives.

First, a UN sponsored declaration of water as an Earth resource that needs to be conserved and its use regulated by a code that is ethical, equitable and ecologically intelligent. This declaration should be by way of a global aspiration which recognises the sovereignty of nation states over their water resources but presses on them a hydro-ethic and a hydro-equity which is against water wastage, water pollution, water degradation, and water-denial and is for water conservation in all its forms.

Second, a beginning towards an international covenant on the uses and abuses of river water and ground water on the same lines as the Law of the Sea. If all the countries of the world can agree to be bound to a law that tells them only that much and no more of the sea is theirs, why should it be unthinkable that some norms be laid down for non sea water?

Third, a Pugwash-equivalent for water which works like a gad-fly goading countries and society at large to honour the declaration and warns them about the hydro-crisis, not just hydro-diplomatically but hydro-normatively and hydro-philosophically. If scientists can raise their voice against the spoliation of Planet Earth by nuclear weapons and actually make difference, winning the Nobel Peace Prize in the process, why cannot the same be done to guard the earth's most precious resource, water?

Fourth—and this may strike all of you as being over the top but, believe me, it is not—a water code for our future in and with outer space. Shakespeare talks of the moon as having water- in fact, of the moon being watery. The greatest of these descriptions occurs in 'Macbeth': "Upon the corner of the moon there hangs a vaporous drop profound". NASA's radar aboard, with 10 other instruments, on India's space vessel Chandrayaana I gave us images of the moon's watery surface.

It is only natural for a species that has colonised its rivers and is draining and muddying them to reach out to and clutch at moon-water for survival. And yet, I put it to you, is there not something 'yuck' about seeking to appropriate what is of value 'out there' merely because it is unguarded?

Will the watery moon's hidden or open lakes have extraction units put up by hydro-technology alongside, drills be bored into them, pumps installed, temporary storage arranged, then low weight bottling be done in some assembly-line technology, all without the support of gravity, and the pure aqua be lifted and removed for consumption by a thirsty earth through the agencies of the techno-market? And will that not generate ferocious competition among the hydro-giants of the world?

Believe me, this is not fantasy. Many under 30s present here may well see bottled moon-water. And I for one would think that a form of hydro-colonisation of outer space.

Fifth and finally, IUCN 's water interventions must include a major and momentous initiative towards suggesting a new hydro-zoning for the world. When I was at school, the geography class map that said 'Rivers of India' had lines on them that looked either like my mother's wavy hairpins or like my own palms with far too many zigzag lines going from everywhere to everywhere, the Ganga resembling the Head Line, the Yamuna just below it saying 'me too', and though their being several riverine claimants to India's footloose Fate Line, none flowing clearly from the North East to South to make up India's Life Line. No attempt was made to explain why some rivers or lines flew west to east, some east to west or meandered, like the amazing trans-Asian Indus and the Brahmaputra, huge distances to drain exhausted; one into the Arabian Sea and another, after losing its identity in other flows, into the Bay of Bengal. Why did we have rivers, riverbeds, floods, flood plains, why was there this thing called a river basin, was never well explained. We were to mark the rivers on a blank map, and we all ended up by doing from the sea end, up to the catchments. No one seemed to regard that as stupid. The IUCN has assigned to certain forms of wildlife an IUCN status such as 'Endangered/I', 'Vulnerable/II', 'Lower risk/II'. Depending on who we are talking about and where, including the individual citizen, a dissident threatened by extremists, we can categorise them as 'Endangered', 'Vulnerable', 'At Risk'.

We need a hydro-zoning that tells the whole world about its water risks and tells it to them 'red hot'. The world needs to be awakened to the horrors its greed have created.

A new hydro-cartography and a new hydro-wisdom must back hydro-diplomacy to address river water issues and to face the larger water crisis that looms overhead and under our feet. We need in fact a hydro-ethic, a hydro-morality, a hydro-philosophy of the highest kind. If IUCN catalyses that it will deserve more than a Nobel Peace Prize, it will deserve the gratitude of Planet Earth.

✧

Poor supply!
WATER SHARING IDEAS

HYDRO ETHICS
HYDRO PHILOSOPHY
HYDRO CALLOUSNESS
HYDRO INTELLIGENCE
HYDRO COMMON SENSE
HYDRO RIGHTS
HYDRO POLITICS
HYDRO SOCIOLOGY
HYDRO COMPETITION
HYDRO SOLIDARITY
HYDRO DIPLOMACY
HYDRO PERSUASION
HYDRO LOGIC

SHARING WATER
ACROSS BORDERS

Water without Borders: Sharing the Flows?

Benedito Braga

AS TRANS-BOUNDARY watercourses keep flowing across borders, men living on separate sides of frontiers still share a common destiny. With 40 per cent of humanity relying on its neighbours to meet its daily needs and their use of water for development, the solutions have to be regional as rivers embody interdependences from the source to the mouth of a river.

If water is stored upstream for irrigation, the flows downstream for agriculture may be less than downstream users are expecting. Whenever a river is contaminated, pollution always flows downwards. When a dam is constructed, benefits are generated but at the same time change of flow regime will impact downstream users. Such examples may explain why the word "rival" comes from the Latin *"rivalis"* meaning one using the same river as another. Within this context, diplomatic negotiations for water sharing are a fundamental and always conflicting basis of relation between States.

In a century where water security is paramount to ensure socioeconomic development of communities, international agreements become essential to guarantee global solutions for a binding resource. Diplomatic agreements established for trans-boundary water management follow conflicting doctrines. Most of these frameworks tend to favor the country which has elaborated it for its own benefit. Like any other social, economic, geopolitical and environmental issues, the solutions require that the parties involved will give-up some benefits to receive others for the good of the watercourse.

Water as a mobile resource is usually considered from different perspectives that face one another: those who give and those who receive. Downstream countries use the principle of 'absolute territorial integrity', such as Egypt, which indicates that downstream riparian countries have the right to receive the natural flow from upstream. In this way, upstream countries are expected to let the natural amount of water flow downstream.

On the other side, upstream countries like Ethiopia base their claims on the 'absolute territorial sovereignty' principle so they may use the right to do whatever they want with the water running through their country regardless of its effects for neighbours.

Finally, some States favour a practical approach by granting the right of using water to the first State which started exploiting the land and consequently the water. Despite these differences of opinions, every State tends to grant a "territorialised" vision of water they may tap.

Anyhow, riparian States must enlarge their scale of assessment for better water management. The purpose of diplomacy is to set a common ground for joint management of rivers and tackle with constraints such as weak political leadership, overlapping claims or non-participation of indispensable States to basin management initiatives. The only way to avoid risks of water scarcity and preventing conflicts is to make water a peace factor. To establish trans-boundary water management, diplomatic efforts must bring the concerned stakeholders to elaborate priorities and shared commitments.

During the past decades successful examples have been implemented by finding common interests either for producing energy, improving irrigation or more generally for economic growth, social welfare and environmental protection.

The Itaipu dam is a great example as it solved a diplomatic impasse involving Brazil and Paraguay. Since the 18th century the two countries had a contentious regarding the ownership of lands in the region of the Seven Falls (now covered by the lake formed by the dam). In the 1960s when the discovery of Rio Parana's hydroelectric potential was made, the two governments made a wise choice: to unite forces and make cooperation prevail. As the need for water for drinking, irrigation and industrial use became urgent, politics conflicted with economics. At that time Brazil and Paraguay were suffering from droughts.

The process began with diplomatic talks between both countries. Initially the goal was to improve the use of water for irrigation of crops. In 1966, the Act of Iguaçu was signed. The agreement made between Brazil and Paraguay was to create a stable supply of hydropower for both countries. Electricity would be divided equally, but Paraguay would be required to repay Brazil for financial assistance within 50 years by selling its surplus power only to Brazil.

In 1973, the Treaty of Itaipu was signed and the construction of the dam started two years later. In 1983, the first generator was operational. Today, the dam provides the 75 per cent of Paraguay's needs of electricity and meets about 25 per cent of Brazil's demands. To ensure success, the Treaty created a bi-national entity with two headquarters established in Brasilia and Asuncion, having an equal representation on the governing council, by sharing equally the produced electricity and exempting taxes for construction materials and energy production.

On a larger scale, water has been considered as the backbone of a peace and development process in South-East Asia. Great diplomatic efforts have led to the constitution of the Mekong River Commission, an intergovernmental body in charge of using water and related resources for mutual benefits. Launched in 1957, the function of Mekong Committee was to give financial and technical support to development projects, including dam construction. During the first years, the committee consisted of Cambodia, Laos, Thailand and South Viet Nam. The committee produced extensive data on basin hydrology, engineering studies, as well as social and economic aspects of water resources.

In April 1995, Cambodia, Laos, Thailand and Viet Nam signed an agreement on "The cooperation for the sustainable development of the Mekong River Basin". This agreement gave birth to the Mekong River Commission which replaced the Mekong Committee. The four countries saw a common interest in jointly managing their shared water resources and developing the economic potential of the river.

The Mekong River Commission is now supporting a basin wide planning programme with the four countries, which is the basis of its 'Integrated Water Resources Development Programme'. This enlarged approach has led the Commission to be also involved in fisheries management, navigation, irrigation, flood management and exploring hydropower possibilities. China, at the beginning of this committee was not a member, is now an observer with voice and fully participates in all meetings of the Mekong Commission.

As the Mekong river example speaks for itself, the greatest asset of a multinational approach is to implement an integrated water management programme. But the more stakeholders you have, the harder it is to find consensus.

The Danube River flows through 14 countries in Central Europe within a basin of 19 countries. The protection of environment and biodiversity has been one of the most important elements on the political agenda of the different Danubian States.

In 1991, after the breakup of USSR, riparian States elaborated a plan for protecting the water quality of the Danube. With the elaboration of the 'Environmental Program for the Danube River Basin' the concerned countries agreed to define common guidelines and monitoring tools for the protection of the river.

In 1998, the International Commission for the Protection of the Danube River was established, consisting of 14 states and the European Union. Its goal is to implement the 'Danube River Protection Convention' by promoting and coordinating sustainable and equitable water management, including conservation and rational use of water and the implementation of the EU Water Framework Directive. The principle of "participation" was taken very seriously in this process. Political and public participation were made at four levels: international, national, regional and local.

Despite the difficulties for cooperating among the large number of States within the Danube region, important progresses have been made as the quality of water has improved. The use of international alarms is an important accomplishment as the 2010 aluminum outbreak in Ajka in Hungary was handled on time.

The complexity of borders, population growth and governance add pressure on shared water users and require sustainable and peaceful solutions. If riparian States agree on joint management frameworks before any conflicts, the economic, social and environmental outputs are much greater than a strictly "territorialised" approach. Research and case studies show us that water conflicts may be prevented through diplomacy in order to improve regional collaboration, civil society involvement and capacity building at all scales by creating an environment of peace rather than conflict.

✧

AS YOU CAN SEE, OUR MEETING ON WATER SHARING JUST CONCLUDED...
TV

HYDRO ETHICS
HYDRO PHILOSOPHY
HYDRO CALLOUSNESS
HYDRO INTELLIGENCE
HYDRO COMMON SENSE
HYDRO RIGHTS
HYDRO POLITICS
HYDRO SOCIOLOGY
HYDRO COMPETITION
HYDRO SOLIDARITY
HYDRO DIPLOMACY
HYDRO PERSUASION
HYDRO LOGIC

SHARING WATER ACROSS BORDERS

Hydrosolidarity and its Place in International Water Diplomacy

Robert G. Varady, Andrea K. Gerlak, and Emily D. McGovern

Introduction

From the earliest written records, dating at least as far back as Kautilya's 4th century BCE manual of statecraft, the Arthashastra, diplomacy has been understood as the art of conducting international relations. Now, as then, this practice includes negotiating alliances, treaties and agreements on behalf of a nation's core interests. These interests nearly always include national security, and commonly encompass territory, populations and resources. Among those resources, water has played a prominent role historically, serving as a boundary, navigational conduit and supply for agriculture and sustenance. When, as frequently happens, water crosses or defines international frontiers, its worth increases and its diplomatic importance grows. Accordingly, "hydro-diplomacy" can be seen as the water-related analogue or a subset of the larger notion of diplomacy. Thus understood, hydro-diplomacy refers to those aspects of water that are subject to international relations—including negotiation of differences and conflict, establishment of specialised transnational institutions, and establishment of protocols and agreements on use.

Although at one extreme, diplomacy can include bullying and ultimately waging war, at the other extreme, it can favour suasion, accommodation, and other techniques that avoid arousing hostility. In a parallel manner, water diplomacy features contrasting approaches to negotiating national interests. One pole is the concept of "hydro-hegemony," which as the term implies features unequal power relationships such as upstream-downstream interactions between states. Its opposite pole, "hydro-solidarity," comprises an approach that self-consciously eschews confrontation and seeks harmonious accord—at watershed levels, as well as at broader national and regional levels.

Since its formulation in the late 1990s, the concept of hydro-solidarity has been embraced and applied by an array of scholars and practitioners. Hydro-solidarity, as intended by its framers, is an ethically driven construct whose final objective is to improve water management. It seeks to advance coordinated management, encourage greater stakeholder participation, integrate diverse interests, assure access to information, enhance equitable access to water, and improve its quality—and at bottom, promote just, inter-institutional cooperation as the chief means to avoid or resolve conflict.

In this paper, we aim to explore the concept of hydro-solidarity and its underlying goals and to relate this to the characteristics of the broader term, hydro-diplomacy. We build from our earlier research investigating the role of hydro-solidarity in global water governance (Gerlak et al., 2009; 2011). First, we outline the concept of hydro-solidarity and how it has evolved over time. Second, we describe how the concept has been applied and utilised by various international organisations as a framework to guide workshops, improve public participation, inform scientific and technical research, and shape donor funding; in this realm, perhaps most notably, hydro-solidarity has been a cornerstone of discussions at recent World Water Forums. Next, we explore linkages between hydro-solidarity and other concepts, such as hydro-hegemony, hydro-ecology, and integrated water resources management (IWRM). Then, we propose some next steps in the realisation of hydro-solidarity as a means to achieve better integrated, more effective, and more ethically driven governance and water management. Finally, we draw some conclusions and consider the significance of hydro-diplomacy in a world whose limited freshwater resources are coming under multiple stresses.

Genesis and Evolving Conceptions of Hydro-solidarity

The term hydro-solidarity was formally articulated by Swedish hydrologist Malin Falkenmark and colleagues at the 1996 IUCN World Conservation Congress (UN Bibliographic Information System, 2009). Later, with Carl Folke, she explained hydro-solidarity as the reconciliation of conflicts of interest in the context of water with a solidarity-based balancing of human livelihood interests, which should be achieved against unavoidable environmental consequences (Falkenmark and Folke, 2002). They deliberately injected an ethical dimension in the eco-hydrological catchment system, requiring "an improved understanding, often site-specific, of the inter-dependencies between hydrological flows and ecosystem processes and dynamics" as well as "proper attention to the hungry and poor, upstream and downstream, to descendants, and to sites and habitats that need to be protected" (Falkenmark and Folke, 2002: 8, 1, respectively). Falkenmark et al. (2004: 219) suggested that guidelines for hydro-solidarity will have to be developed on "principles of human rights, fairness, equity, and equality principles" through a process that incorporates adaptation in water and ecosystem management.

With the passage of time, the term hydro-solidarity acquired greater specificity, only to be later enlarged and rendered more vague. In 2003, during his keynote address at the 11th World Congress of the International Water Resources Association in Madrid, William Cosgrove, a former vice president of the World Bank and past president of the World Water Council, defined hydro-solidarity as "decision-making surrounding the management of water in a basin; between those living upstream and downstream, between urban and rural dwellers, between human needs and environmental sustainability" (Cosgrove, 2003: 530). A year later, with considerably greater detail, geochemist Wim Salomons (2004: 8) defined hydrosolidarity as: "a full upstream/downstream integration of monitoring, stakeholder consultation, models and expert systems that can link basin pressure to transfers, across various administrative and/or political boundaries, and between the various land users, water users and other stakeholders."

By 2006, however, references to hydro-solidarity as "the wider vision seeking higher levels of ethical involvement from citizens with regard to their interactions with water in order to ensure peace and coexistence" (Netherlands Foundation for Water and Climate, 2006: 6) would seem to have reverted to the term's original, more humanistic—and perhaps more idealistic and less easily applicable—sense.

At the centre of global water governance discussions, the Stockholm International Water Institute (SIWI) notes that the term has come to have several distinct, often simultaneous, definitions in practice (SIWI, 2010a). At the lowest scale, the catchment level, hydro-solidarity refers to ethically integrated land, water, and ecosystem management. At the national scale, hydro-solidarity may be achieved by intra-national water transfers from water-abundant to water-short regions. Regionally and globally, it may be achieved through the transfer of virtual water as part of a larger food security strategy. And at the cross-national scale, hydro-solidarity may be realised by upstream/downstream water sharing in international river basins.

Applications and Utility

Since Falkenmark first articulated hydrosolidarity in 1996, the term has appeared frequently in journals, seminars, global and regional councils, and research workshops. SIWI has played a historic and significant role in the proliferation of the concept, serving as the chief platform for promoting the term through its many events. For example, SIWI conference and workshop papers often apply hydro-solidarity concepts to particular river basins and watersheds (Duchovny, 2002). Van der Zaag (2007) explores how critical institutional interdependencies that exist within shared catchment areas and river basins in South Africa could foster hydro-solidarity. Similarly, Kemerink et al. (2009) explore the potential of hydro-solidarity as a mechanism to reconcile disputes over water in the Pangani River basin in northern Tanzania. These examples provide instances of how hydro-solidarity has been applied to frame water governance in order to improve water management.

Across the globe, other international institutions and scientific research gatherings have employed the concept of hydrosolidarity. The United Nations Environment Programme has stressed managing fisheries in river basins based on hydro-solidarity between stakeholders (UNEP, 2002). Elsewhere, the Interstate Commission for Water Coordination in Central Asia, has identified public participation as central to hydro-solidarity in its region (ICWC, 2005).The Global Environment Facility, a major funding agency, has stressed the importance of linkages between freshwater and oceans as a necessary step to achieving hydro-solidarity (GEF, 2006). And the Organization of American States has linked hydro-solidarity to integrated water resources management in an effort to promote the development of national water plans (OAS, 2006). The term has also been a focus for several World Water Forums. The 4th World Water Forum in Mexico in 2006, for example, included an agenda to advance the establishment of a local water culture and hydro-solidarity (World Water Forum, 2006). The 5th World Water Forum, held in Istanbul, Turkey, in spring 2009, included a thematic heading titled "Managing and Protecting Water Resources and their Supply Systems to Meet Human and Environmental Needs," in which participants discussed hydro-solidarity as the mechanism to improve cooperation in a river basin context (World Water Forum, 2009).

Although there does not as yet exist a national water code or international water treaty referring explicitly to hydro-solidarity, water scholars and decision-makers continue to reference and utilise the term. This is in part because the notion helps organise thinking about water ethics, even if it is difficult to operationalise. The features of hydro-solidarity based on its multiple applications include use of the concept to indicate broad cooperation or solidarity around water resources. Its practical, applied features emphasise coordinated management, equitable allocation and access, ethical decision-making, and greater stakeholder participation. Hydro-solidarity is progressively becoming an international reference point and a component of "soft law."

Linkages to Related Concepts: Hydro-hegemony, Hydro-ecology and IWRM

In addition to its potential role in supporting non-confrontational efforts of hydro-diplomacy, hydro-solidarity has kinship with a number of other commonly used terms (see Figure 1).On the opposite pole, hydro-hegemony, as noted, refers to the exercise of hegemonic power in trans-boundary water interaction (SIWI, 2010b; Rasheed, 2003). The concept is utilised in analysing trans-boundary water conflicts via explorations of power imbalances among states—the very imbalances which hydro-solidarity seeks to redress (Zeitoun and Warner, 2006).

A strikingly similar paradigm to hydro-solidarity is hydro-ecology. Hydro-ecology (or eco-hydrology) is considered by its proponents at UNESCO's International Hydrology Programme to be a new integrative science that seeks solutions to issues surrounding water, people and the environment (Zalewski et al., 1997; IHP, 2007). It emphasises the hydrological cycle and its effects on ecological processes and human well-being (Rodríguez-Iturbe, 2000; Vwery, 2003; Breshears, 2005; Wood et al., 2008). (Note that the journal Ecohydrology stresses ecological and hydrological interconnections but is less concerned with the human well-being notion that seems to be central to UNESCO's hydro-ecology concept.) As the hydro-solidarity and hydro-ecology terms have evolved, both embrace the importance of integrated management, inter-disciplinarity and catchment-scale approaches, and link these to a set of ethical principles.

Hydro-solidarity is also becoming inextricably linked to IWRM. Defined as the coordinated management of water, land and related resources, IWRM has often been presented as an operational means to achieve sustainable water policies (Allan, 2006; Mukhtarov, 2008; Trottier, 2008). One of the features of IWRM most relevant to hydro-solidarity is its emphasis on a participatory approach that stresses local knowledge and joint learning processes (Mostert et al., 2008). With this linkage to IWRM around participation, a narrower interpretation of hydro-solidarity is emerging—one that emphasises an "integrated" approach to managing water resources and relies heavily on stakeholder input and coordination (GWP, 2003; World Water Forum, 2009; Larson, n.d.). In this way, hydro-solidarity is becoming shaped by (and adopted because of) this emphasis on integration—thereby, appearing to mirror the principal aims of IWRM. This narrower version of hydro-solidarity reinforces earlier notions of the concept that frame it as arguably the best approach to achieving cooperative and unified management in trans-boundary settings (Lundqvist, 1999; Lundqvist and Falkenmark, 2000; Wouters, 2000; SIWI, 2001). In any event, Falkenmark's conceptualisation of hydro-solidarity has evolved beyond the management and technical-oriented focus of IWRM to represent more of an "all encompassing, multi-dimensional guiding ethic for solving water-related problems" (Falkenmark, 2005: 40).

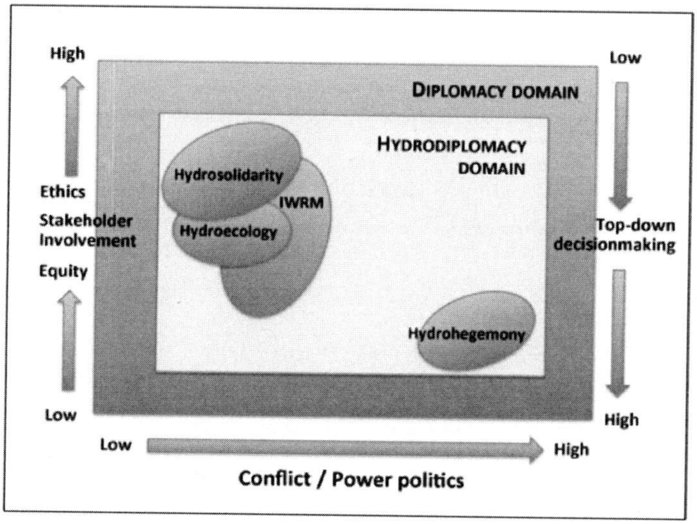

Hydro-solidarity and Related Concepts

Next Steps

How precisely does one know hydro-solidarity when one sees it? Some economists and engineers argue that effective use of the concept requires the development of benchmarks or indicators for achieving and maintaining hydro-solidarity (Gerlak et al., 2009: 315). Policy and economic scholars, by contrast, have emphasised the overarching need for good governance. They have suggested that while striving toward hydro-solidarity may be beneficial, the approach still requires fundamental water laws and policies, and further necessitates practices to be successfully funded, implemented, maintained and monitored (Wouters, 2000; Jagerskog, 2002; Wouters, 2010). And recognising that upstream users are unlikely to give up their interests for the benefit of downstream users without compensation, these observers have noted that appropriate incentives need to be developed. Such incentives may include innovative taxation policies or establishment of other benefits, such as financing of investments or provision of non-related goods and services (Castelain, 2002; Bayarsaihan and McKinney, 2004).

New tools—like the ecosystem-services approach in which catchments are viewed as assets that deliver water and ecological goods and services—may be a helpful step (Falkenmark and Folke, 2002). Because interstate relations along watercourses generally are seen as zero-sum games between upstream and downstream riparians, an ecosystem-services approach could highlight positive externalities as well, promoting cooperation and solidarity between the concerned states (Lopez-Hoffman et al., 2009). Proposed actions and decisions could be evaluated against an environmental axis—for example, based on the functions of water—to implement better ethics around water. Proponents of hydro-solidarity envision it as an all-encompassing, multi-dimensional guiding ethic (Falkenmark, 2005). But to truly capture the complex realities of water-sharing practices and their inherent asymmetrical distributions of power, those who utilise hydro-solidarity must embrace the dynamic and context-specific conditions of water use (Kemerink et al., 2009).

Conclusions

Evolving conceptions of hydro-solidarity—and how exactly to forge it—have begun to penetrate the broader conversation about how to resolve trans-boundary water dilemmas. Over the past two decades, various international organisations, scholars, practitioners, and even decision-makers have advanced the concept of hydro-solidarity as a means to call for ethically motivated, equitable participation, integration and interstate cooperation.

Increasingly, hydro-solidarity is becoming linked to other, related concepts in water governance such as eco-hydrology. Significantly, there have been palpable signs that hydro-solidarity is being embraced as a vehicle to achieve IWRM. To better realise hydro-solidarity requires the appropriate benchmarks and indicators; effective, new policy instruments and incentives; and innovative changes in water laws and policies. The ecosystem-services approach holds particular promise in the realisation of hydro-solidarity.

With population pressures, urbanisation, economic development and global environmental change driving increased demand for freshwater, diplomacy will be called on increasingly to anticipate, mitigate and resolve conflicting claims on shared water resources. Nowhere will this contest be more stark than in trans-boundary regions, where bordering states will need to balance national interests with regional welfare and economic security. Therein lies the great challenge of hydro-diplomacy and the concomitant potential of hydro-solidarity.

Acknowledgments

The present paper relies heavily on two previously published articles on the same subject. The first (Gerlak et al., 2009) appeared in International Negotiation; the second (Gerlak et al., 2011) was published in Water International. We are grateful for the contributions of two co-authors of those publications, Arin Haverland and Olivier Petit. We also acknowledge long-term financial support from the Morris K. and Stewart L. Udall Foundation, the U.S. National Oceanic and Atmospheric Administration, and the Inter-American Institute for Global Change Research; and a close collaborative relationship with UNESCO's International Hydrological Programme. Finally, we wish to recognise the seminal thinking of Prof Malin Falkenmark, whose conceptualisation of hydro-solidarity was the starting point for our explorations of that notion.

References

Allan, J.A. (2006). *"IWRM: The new sanctioned discourse"*, in P.P. Mollinga, A. Dixit and K. Athukorala (eds.), *IWRM in South Asia: Global Theory, Emerging Practice and Local Needs*. New Delhi: Sage. pp.38–63.

Bayarsaihan, T. and D. McKinney (eds.) (2004). *Water for All: Past Experiences and Future Challenges Cooperation in Shared Water Resources in Central Asia.* Manila: Asian Development Bank.

Breshears, D.B. (2005). *"An ecologist's perspective of ecohydrology"*, Bulletin of the Ecological Society of America 86: 296–300.

Castelain, S. (2002). *Proceedings of From Conflict to Co-operation in International Water Resources Management: Challenges and Opportunities (International Conference).* November 20–22. Delft: UNESCO-IHE Institute for Water Education.

Cosgrove, W. (2003). *"Fulfilling the world water vision: Hydrosolidarity: A Water Forum Contribution"*, Water International 28 (4): 527–31.

Duchovny, V.A. (2002). *"Big challenges and unlimited opportunities: What are the constraints on cooperation?"*, in Proceedings of From Conflict to Co-operation in International Water Resources Management: Challenges and Opportunities (International Conference). November 20–22. Delft: UNESCO-IHE Institute for Water Education. pp.119–24.

Falkenmark, M. (2005). *Towards hydrosolidarity: Ample opportunities for human ingenuity.* Fifteen Year Message from the Stockholm Water Symposia. Stockholm: Stockholm International Water Institute.

Falkenmark, M. and C. Folke (2002). *"The ethics of socio-ecohydrological catchment management: Towards hydrosolidarity"*, Hydrology and Earth System Sciences 6 (1): 1–9.

Falkenmark, M., J. Rockström and N. Tolba (2004). *Balancing Water for Humans and Nature: The New Approach in Ecohydrology.* London: Earthsan.

Gerlak, A., R.G. Varady and A. Haverland (2009). *"Hydrosolidarity and international water conflict"*, International Negotiation 14 (2): 311-28. Special issue. *"Negotiating International River Disputes to Avert Conflict & Facilitate Cooperation,"* A. Gerlak and N. Zawahari, eds.

Global Environment Facility (GEF) (2006). *International Workshop on Freshwater Coastal Marine Management Inter-linkages: Final Report.* Mexico City, January 10-11. Presented by the Global Forum on Ocean, Coasts and Islands, GEF. IOC/UNESCO and UNEP/GPA.

Gerlak, A., R.G. Varady, O. Petit and A. Haverland (2011). *"Hydrosolidarity and beyond: Can ethics and equity find a place in today's water resource management?"*, Water International 36(3): 251–65.

Global Water Partnership (GWP) (2003). *Water Management and Ecosystems: Living with Change.* Stockholm.

International Hydrological Programme (IHP) (2007). *What is ecohydrology?* Ecohydrology Programme. Available from: http://typo38.unesco.org/en/ecohydrology.html [Accessed 17 May 2007].

Interstate Commission for Water Coordination in Central Asia (ICWC) (2005). *Challenges and Actions for Integrated Approaches. Regional Working Group under Coordination, Global Water Partnership Central Asia and Caucasus.* Available from: http://www.cawater- info.net/4wwf/pdf/ca_position_paper_eng.pdf [last accessed 1 June 2011].

Jagerskog, A. (2002). *"Contributions of regime theory in understanding interstate water cooperation: Lessons learned in the Jordan River Basin*", in A. Turton and R. Henwood (eds.), Hydropolitics in the Developing World: A South African Perspective. Pretoria: African Water Issues Research Unit. pp.73–78.

Kautilya (1923). *Kautilya'sArthashastra.* Translated by R. Shamasastry. 2nd ed. Mysore: Wesleyan Mission Press.

Kemerink, J.S., R. Ahlers and P. van der Zaag (2009). *"Assessment of the potential for hydro-solidarity within plural legal conditions of traditional irrigation systems in northern Tanzania"*, Physics and Chemistry of the Earth 34(13–16): 881–89.

Larson, K.L. (n.d.). *"Hydrosolidarity"*, in Water Encyclopedia [online].
Available from: http://www.waterencyclopedia.com/Hy-La/Hydrosolidarity.html#ixzz0UVzlSwZ4/.

Lopez-Hoffman, L., E. McGovern, R.G. Varady and K. W. Flessa (eds.) (2009). *Conservation of Shared Environments: Learning from the United States and Mexico.* Tucson, AZ: University of Arizona Press.

Lundqvist, J. (1999). *"Towards upstream/downstream hydrosolidarity"*, Water International 24 (3): 275–77.
Lundqvist, J. and M. Falkenmark (2000). *"Drainage basin morphology: A starting point for balancing water needs, land use and fishery protection"*, Fisheries Management and Ecology 7: 1–14.

Mostert, E., M. Craps and C. Pahl-Wostl (2008). *"Social learning: The key to integrated water resources management"*, Water International 33 (3): 293–304.

Mukhtarov, F.G. (2008). *"Intellectual history and current status of integrated water resources management: A global perspective"*, in C. Pahl-Wostl, P. Kabat and J. Möltgen (eds.), Adaptive and Integrated Water Management: *Coping with Complexity and Uncertainty.* Berlin: Springer. pp.167–185.

Netherlands Foundation on Water and Climate (2006). Cooperative program on water and climate: Netherlands. January News. Delft: Netherlands Foundation on Water and Climate.

Organization of American States (OAS) (2006). Preparatory workshop on integrated water resources management to develop national integrated water resources management plans. Quito. June 19–20.

Rasheed, K.B.S. (2003). "Hydro-hegemony: India's inter-basin water transfer plan threatens our eco-existence", *The Daily Star* [online]. Available from: http://www.thedailystar.net/2003/10/07/d31007150188.htm/.

Rodríguez-Iturbe, I. (2000). "Ecohydrology: A hydrologic perspective of climate–soil–vegetation dynamics", Water Resources Research 36 (10): 3–9.

Salomons, W. (2004). *European Catchments: Catchment Changes and Their Impact on the Coast.* Amsterdam: Institute for Environmental Studies, VrijeUniversiteit.

Stockholm International Water Institute (SIWI) (2001). *Water Security for Cities, Food and Environment: Towards Catchment Hydrosolidarity.* Stockholm: SIWI.

Stockholm International Water Institute (SIWI) (2010a). *"New knowledge areas: Hydrosolidarity"*. Available at: http://www.siwi.org/knowledge/new/.

Stockholm International Water Institute (SIWI) (2010b). *"New knowledge areas: Hydro-hegemony"*. Available at: http://www.siwi.org/knowledge/new/

Trottier, J. (2008). *"Water crises: Political construction or physical reality?"*, Contemporary Politics 14 (2): 197–214.

UN Bibliographic Information System (2009). Hydrosolidarity.

United Nations Environment Programme (UNEP) (2002). Atlas of International Freshwater Agreements. Nairobi: UNEP.

Van der Zaag P. (2007). *"Asymmetry and equity in water resources management; critical institutional issues for Southern Africa"*, Water Resource Management 21: 1993–2004.

Vwery, S. (2003). A Hydrosolidarity and Watershed Management Roundtable Report. No. 14. Colombo: International Water Management Institute.

Wood, P.J., D.M. Hannah and J.P. Sadler (eds.) (2008). *Hydroecology and Ecohydrology: Past, Present and Future.*

Chichester: John Wiley & Sons Ltd.

World Water Forum (2006)."Thematic Area 5", in 4th World Water Forum Framework for Baseline Document 2005, Risk Management. Available from: http://www.worldwaterforum4.org.mx/uploads/TBL_DOCS_107_35.pdf. [accessed 31 May 2010]

World Water Forum (2009). *"Session 3.1.1: Boundless basins: What are the successes and failures of hydro-solidarity?"*, in 5th World Water Forum. Istanbul. Available from: http://portal.worldwaterforum5.org/wwf5/en-us/themes/Theme3/Topic3.1/Pages/default.aspx/.

Wouters, P. (2000). *"The relevance and role of water law in the sustainable development of fresh-water: Replacing 'hydro-sovereignty' with 'hydro-solidarity' and horizontal solutions"*, Water International 25 (2): 202–07.

Wouters, P. (2010).Water Security: Global, Regional and Local Challenges. London: Institute for Public Policy Research.

Zalewski, M., G.A. Janauer and G. Jolankai (1997). *"Ecohydrology: A new paradigm for the sustainable use of aquatic resources"*, UNESCO IHP Technical Document in Hydrology No. 7: IHP – V Projects 2.3/2.4. Paris: UNESCO.

Zeitoun, M. and J. Warner (2006). *"Hydrohegemony: A framework for analysis of transboundary water conflicts"*, Water Policy 8 (5): 435–60.

INTERNATIONAL
NATIONAL
REGIONAL
LOCAL
Rustam

HYDRO ETHICS
HYDRO PHILOSOPHY
HYDRO CALLOUSNESS
HYDRO INTELLIGENCE
HYDRO COMMON SENSE
HYDRO RIGHTS
HYDRO POLITICS
HYDRO SOCIOLOGY
HYDRO COMPETITION
HYDRO SOLIDARITY
HYDRO DIPLOMACY
HYDRO PERSUASION
HYDRO LOGIC

SHARING WATER ACROSS BORDERS

Water Diplomacy: Bringing Diplomacy into Water Cooperation and Water into Diplomacy

Marko Keskinen, Antti Inkinen, Ulla Hakanen, Antti Rautavaara and Markku Niinioja

WATER IS a critical prerequisite for any human activity and its management is key for sustainable development. Food and energy security, recognition of water and sanitation as human rights, poverty eradication, health, women's rights and gender equality, equitable social and economic development all depend on responsible planning and use of this vital element. Investments in water management are at the core of any society's ability for economic development and improvement of the well-being of its citizens. At the same time, population growth, urbanization, changing consumption and production patterns, climate change and degradation of surface and ground waters all enhance the pressures to our water resources. It is thus no wonder that the role of water as a strategic natural resource has increased in relevance and urgency, with competing interests related to its use locally, nationally, regionally and internationally.

Water usage priorities in different parts of a shared water body can differ greatly and sometimes impose limitations on each other. The differing demands and concerns that different parties have on water resources are understandable and legitimate. Yet, as water commonly crosses multiple administrative boundaries, water management should be considered as a joint task between these different actors both within and between the countries. The mechanisms facilitating cooperation on water management and reconciliation of the differing interests related to water use must therefore be promoted and strengthened. Particularly critical this is in the multi-country settings, including different kinds of transboundary waters from surface waters such as rivers and lakes to aquifers and all the way to coastal and marine ecosystems.

The broad concept of hydro-diplomacy – or water diplomacy as we prefer to call it instead of more technical 'hydro' – provides one interesting mechanism for this. Yet, as every context is different, we see that water diplomacy cannot build on some certain, predefined procedures, but should rather be seen as a broad process that shares some common characteristics. For this reason, it is also useful to share ideas and experiences on what water diplomacy could be and what it should achieve. Here comes our take on it.

Water diplomacy vs. water cooperation

How does water diplomacy differ from the more commonly used concept of (transboundary) water cooperation? There is, after all, a plethora of documents written, experience gained and methods proposed for water cooperation in various settings.

For us, water diplomacy and water cooperation are closely intertwined. Yet, while they are sometimes considered even synonymous, we see them to be clearly differing processes with differing characteristics. Most remarkably, we see that water diplomacy focuses on the political aspects of transboundary water management and related cooperation. Depending on the context, such aspects can mean different things. In some settings, the politics rule over all other aspects of joint water management, hindering cooperation. In other settings, water cooperation may be too non-political: political tensions may not be duly taken into account and the cooperation focuses only on physical and/or technical aspects of joint water resources. In both settings, water diplomacy can play a vital role in addressing the political aspects, thus also facilitating and even enabling cooperation.

In simple terms, water diplomacy can thus be seen as a political extension of water cooperation, being particularly useful in situations where cooperation is laden with competing interests, political agendas and even mistrust between the parties. Whereas water cooperation builds – and depends – on the idea of collaboration, water diplomacy has quite commonly as its starting point weak or even non-existing cooperation. In this way, one of the main goals of water diplomacy may simply be the establishment of functioning process for water cooperation. Allocation and timing of water cooperation as such, can be seen as one instrument of water diplomacy.

The processes of water diplomacy are likely to exist in the contexts of already existing water cooperation as well. They can be an integral and visible part of cooperation mechanisms (e.g. regular multi-country negotiations) and/or then 'hidden' negotiations and deliberations between some or all parties of the cooperation. In this way, water diplomacy may be the largely invisible but nevertheless critical ingredient of water cooperation, enabling the discussion on particularly contentious issues that could otherwise hinder the actual cooperation.

It must also be noted that water diplomacy should not been considered as a synonym to dispute settlement or crisis management. As any diplomacy, also water diplomacy refers to the conduct of international relations in broad terms, aiming at promoting good relations, cooperation, peace and prosperity. The desired results of water diplomacy are thus not just related to water cooperation, but extend to, for example, improved regional security and stability, regional integration, improved trade relations and power sharing pools. In this way, the processes of water diplomacy can promote almost any geopolitical improvement in relation between countries that are sharing a joint water body.

Practicing water diplomacy

Given the inherently political nature of water diplomacy, it differs from the traditional processes of water cooperation. How then to practice or at least facilitate water diplomacy? We see that successful water diplomacy requires two critical acknowledgements: Firstly, that there are and will be competing and even conflicting interests towards shared water resources. Secondly, that it is nevertheless beneficial that such competing interests are looked at, negotiated and – ideally – managed jointly, as the non-collaboration is likely to result in worse situation to all parties. Thus, (water) diplomacy should not be perceived solely as protection of one's own interests, but as an ability and willingness to understand and accommodate the needs of others as well. Instead of seeing this as something mutually exclusive, a zero-sum game, shared international waters should rather be seen from a perspective of shared opportunities for positive regional benefits that can exceed the optimum national benefits, for example in the form of energy pools or trade relations. The aim of water diplomacy is therefore to look for and strengthen these mutual benefits in bilateral, regional and international contexts.

From this follows that water diplomacy cannot focus only on water. Instead, we should consider the key water-related sectors, such as energy and food security as well as climate change, population growth and urbanisation as the "hard" drivers of transboundary cooperation as opposed to the sometimes perceived notion of cooperating on "soft" environmental values. This also indicates that it is not enough to bring diplomacy into water cooperation (and hence to talk about water diplomacy), but we should ensure that water is embedded, or mainstreamed in other types of transboundary cooperation, and, consequently, in general diplomatic relations as well. This is crucial as the underlying reasons for disputes and diplomatic tensions seemingly on water, may in fact originate outside the water field.

Indeed, due to the critical role that water has for countries' economies, water may serve as an important catalyst for cooperation. In this way, water cooperation can in some situations emerge as a tool for general diplomacy, providing entry point for collaboration in international relations and regional geopolitics. Such a possibility is particularly interesting in transboundary settings, where water and related natural resources can promote stability, tighter regional cooperation and even integration. An example of such process is the European Union, which emerged from joint management of two critical raw materials, steel and coal.

Conventions and organizations promoting cooperation

Legal initiatives and frameworks can have a major role in facilitating water diplomacy: water cooperation is after all based on common rules and agreements. Particularly the concept of reasonable and equitable utilisation by all riparian states – as recognised already in the 1966 Helsinki Rules on the Uses of Waters of International Rivers and in several regional and international agreements after that – provides a strong and practical guiding principle for all water diplomacy processes.

Finland is a strong supporter of both the 1997 UN Convention on the Law of Non-

Navigational Uses of International Watercourses and the 1992 UNECE Convention on the Protection and Use of Transboundary Watercourses and International Lakes. It was Finland who proposed already in 1970 to the UN that rules for international watercourses should be developed and codified, and the UNECE 1992 Convention was signed in Helsinki, Finland. The 1997 UN Convention still lacks ratifications from coming into force, but thanks to the persistence of international NGOs and academia the pace of new ratifications has again picked up.

The UNECE Convention, in turn, is up and running with active secretariat and other mechanisms of implementation. It is also just about to turn into a global instrument open also for non-UNECE countries. Both of these conventions are framework agreements that can guide the riparian states when discussing and negotiating about the use of shared waters. Such guidance is provided already before ratification, through utilisation of the principles customary international water law included in the agreements. Yet, we see that the ratification of both conventions should be encouraged, and it would also benefit the processes of water diplomacy.

Many water cooperation agreements also have a joint body, such as a river commission, that facilitates the cooperation e.g. by providing technical support and by gathering information. Such body can provide major support also for water diplomacy, as it creates a natural forum for discussion and can generate relevant and jointly produced data and information to facilitate the discussions. There are examples of such joint bodies, in differing stage of maturity, throughout the world, from the Nile to the Mekong.

Water diplomacy actors

While the state actors play commonly a key role in conducting diplomacy, the governments are not the only actors involved in water diplomacy. Similarly to water cooperation, also water diplomacy should be seen as, and is ideally supported through, a multi-tracked approach. In many settings, civil society and/or private sector actors can significantly encourage – although sometimes also discourage – diplomatic processes through their interaction with politicians. They may also have a crucial role domestically, initiating discussion and raising awareness among the general public. Similarly, research institutes and universities can contriburte to water diplomacy by providing objective, transparent information on the benefits and costs of collaboration. All such actors can also collaborate across the national borders, building trust, showing example and sharing best practices. It is also part of water diplomacy to consider how these different elements and tracks can be best used in different settings and geopolitical situation.

UN organisations, development banks, international NGOs as well as development partners all have their role in water diplomacy. External actors can contribute to water diplomacy by bringing in their expertise and (objective) knowledge, and by acting as a facilitator or adviser. International and regional organizations provide also important fora for water diplomacy. For example, side events related to benefits of transboundary water cooperation have become a regular feature in high level meetings.

Way forward

In Finland, water issues are considered as a part of comprehensive foreign and security policy, aiming at strengthening international stability, security, peace, justice and sustainable development as well as promoting the rule of law, democracy and human rights. Promotion of water security at different levels is also the key objective of the International strategy for Finland's Water Sector, published in 2009 jointly by the Finnish Ministry for Foreign Affairs, the Ministry of Agriculture and Forestry and the Ministry of the Environment. Finland promotes transboundary water cooperation actively also within the context of the European Union, both in Europe and globally.

Finland's Development Policy is considered an element of our foreign and security policy. Among its objectives, laid out in the Government Development Policy Program, is the promotion of equitable and sustainable management of water resources, including transboundary waters. Finland supports transboundary cooperation in the Mekong, Central Asia and Nile regions by providing both financial and technical assistance and by engaging in appropriate dialogue platforms with river basin organisations, governments, civil society and other partners. We also promote linkages between water and other sectors, and for example in Mekong our water collaboration is complemented with regional programmes focusing energy and environment. To improve the global scientific base on shared waters, Finland supports the UNEP Transboundary Water Assessment Programme.

Also the recently adopted Government Security and Defence Policy Report addresses availability of clean water as a growing ecological and political challenge, noting that fear for sufficiency of water and poor quality of water resources may lead even to conflicts. At the same time the Report notes that management of shared water resources may help to ease tensions. Ensuring availability of natural resources requires strengthening of rule-based and open cooperation.

In July 2013 the Foreign Affairs Council of the EU adopted Conclusions on EU Water Diplomacy. The aim is to proactively engage in transboundary water security challenges and more effectively promote collaborative and sustainable water management arrangements regionally and globally. In the Conclusions the EU also recognizes the importance of the 1997 UN and 1992 UNECE Conventions. The Council also recognizes the need for coherence and coordination between different political, security, financial, technical, disaster relief and development considerations and activities as a prerequisite for successful water diplomacy.

Water is gaining higher political attention locally, nationally, regionally and globally – as it should be. Importantly, the need for cooperation at different levels is being increasingly acknowledged. There is thus a momentum to promote water diplomacy, which we consider a vital element of water cooperation, particularly in transboundary settings. Both implementation of the decisions of the Rio+20 UN Conference on Sustainable Development and discussions on post-2015 development agenda provide good frameworks for promotion of sustainable and equitable management of water resources. Water diplomacy can also form a critical element of the emerging discussion about water-energy-food nexus, and in general about the (possible) securitization of water and related natural resources.

✧

WATER INFORMATION
Collect it Yourself.
OFFICIAL

HYDRO ETHICS
HYDRO PHILOSOPHY
HYDRO CALLOUSNESS
HYDRO INTELLIGENCE
HYDRO COMMON SENSE
HYDRO RIGHTS
HYDRO POLITICS
HYDRO SOCIOLOGY
HYDRO COMPETITION
HYDRO SOLIDARITY
HYDRO DIPLOMACY
HYDRO PERSUASION
HYDRO LOGIC

SHARING WATER
ACROSS BORDERS

Hydro-diplomacy: The Trans-boundary Dimension of the Water, Energy and Food Security Nexus

Torkil Jønch Clausen and Hanne Bach

The Water and Food Challenge

At the First World Food Summit 1974 the US Secretary of State, Henry Kissinger, said that "no child will go hungry to bed in ten years." Yet, by year 2000 more than 800 million people still would go hungry to bed, and the world adopted a Millennium Development Goal to "reduce hunger by half by 2015." While food production has increased over the past 30 years, we still leave some 1 billion people hungry. International estimates of food demand by 2050 are an increase in the range of 60-70 per cent compared with today, leaving us with a major challenge to feed the world and ensure food security for all. No food can be produced without water, and some 70 per cent of all water withdrawals in the world, and more than 90 per cent of the world consumptive use of water, goes into agriculture, mainly food production. Hence, the world's food security challenge is very much a water challenge as well. With economic and social development, diets are changing towards more meat consumption, which requires 10-20 times more water than the production of grains, and this adds to the water-food challenge.

The Water and Energy Challenge

Another major challenge related to water is energy production, with much the same characteristics as food production in terms of lack of access and growing demands. Today some 1.3 billion people are without access to electricity, and with energy demands estimated to grow by more than 60 per cent over the next 30 years the world faces a major energy security challenge. Again, as with food, energy production is highly dependent on water, for extraction, cooling, bio-fuel production and hydropower generation. In the US and Europe, some 35-45 per cent of all water abstracted is used for energy production, and although the major part of this is for cooling with limited consumptive use, shortage of water, as in drought years, lead to shortages of energy. Worldwide some 7-8 percent of all energy is used for water pumping and treatment. The expected increase in renewable energy production such as bio-fuel in many ways adds to the water-energy challenge.

In the Asia-Pacific Water Development Outlook of 2007 the Prime Minister of India is quoted for stating that, "if all members of society can have adequate access to energy and water, many of the societal problems can be solved".

The Water Challenge

Many parts of the world are already suffering severe water problems, both too much during floods and too little during droughts, and almost 50 per cent of the world population is expected to live under water stress in 2050. Even without the increased pressure from food and energy production, this situation may be seriously aggravated by the impacts of climate change, in terms of long term temperature and hydrologic change, increased variability and sea level rise. With the expected growth in demands for water for food, energy and other societal purposes, we face a challenge of how to manage our water resources wisely to cope with these demands whilst maintaining a healthy environment and a bio-diverse world.

The Water, Energy and Food Security Nexus

While this may sound like doom and gloom, and a world on track towards a water, energy and food crisis, it need not be. With wise governance, new technologies, increased awareness leading to reduced loss and waste of precious water, energy and food, these problems can be solved. Considering that an estimated 40 per cent of all food produced is lost and that extreme differences in both water and energy efficiency exist suggest the positive prospect for finding solutions.

In the run-up to the third world summit on development and environment in Rio in 2012 (Rio+20), the so-called "water, energy and food security nexus" was discussed widely in the international community, starting with the Bonn 2011 Nexus Conference in November 2011 at the initiative of the German Government, and with the support from and participation by the UN systems and a host of countries and international organisations. The nexus approach recognises the links between water, energy and food in analysis, planning, management and implementation, and the need to address the trade- offs and potential impacts on environment, climate, people's livelihoods and other economic sectors.

The Bonn 2011 Conference identified six "nexus opportunities" being: (1) increasing policy coherence by ensuring synergies and trade-offs among water, energy and food security; (2) accelerating access by progressively realising human rights obligations to water, energy and food, (3) creating more with less by increasing resource productivity; (4)ending waste and minimise losses by reducing losses along the supply chains; (5) valuing natural infrastructure by securing, improving and restoring the multi-functional value of biodiversity and ecosystems; and (6) mobilising consumer influence by catalysing the role of individuals in choosing consumption patterns of water, energy and food.

The nexus approach also recognises that the concept of Integrated Water Resources Management (IWRM), building on horizontal integration between sectors and stakeholders, and vertical integration from the smallest watershed to the trans-boundary river basin, as the basis for sound and sustainable water resources management underlying the nexus.

The Trans-boundary Dimension of the Nexus

However, with almost 40 per cent of the world population living in the 263 major trans-boundary river basins of the world, shared by two or more countries, the water, energy and food security challenge calls for solutions and synergies across jurisdictional boundaries. Similar challenges exist across boundaries between states within federations. Hence the nexus has a strong trans-boundary dimension, and vice versa trans-boundary water resources management needs to recognise and address the nexus challenges. This was mentioned, but not properly addressed in Bonn.

In order to address this important dimension of the nexus the Mekong River Commission and the Government of Thailand decided to make a contribution on this issue prior to Rio+20. This "Mekong2Rio" initiative involved some 350 participants, including high level representatives from 14 trans-boundary river basins from all continents of the world, and 16 international organisations meeting in Phuket in April 2012 at the "Mekong2Rio International Conference on Transboundary River Basin Management". It produced a Message to Rio, and a full Mekong2Rio Report that was launched at the World Water Week in Stockholm in August 2012. Some examples of trans-boundary water-energy-food security issues raised in Phuket follow below to illustrate the particular aspects.

Examples of Trans-boundary Nexus Issues

There are numerous examples of regional water- energy cooperation that link upstream hydropower development with downstream power needs, such as in the Mekong, Congo, Nile and Orange Basins, creating regional grids and markets and thus linking national and regional energy policies.

Food security is the overriding agenda in many trans-boundary basins, demonstrated for example by the planned doubling of irrigation in Indus basin and basins in Southern Africa, and a planned six-fold increase of irrigation in the Niger Basin. Worldwide there is still 'development space' in some basins, but serious trade-offs to be made in already fully allocated trans-boundary basins.

An important trans-boundary issue in many basins is the impact of upstream development on downstream fisheries. In the North this is often regarded a biodiversity issue, such as in the Columbia and Danube Basins, while for most basins in the South fish is important for their food security. Upstream hydropower development in the Mekong Basin, for example, poses a major threat to the world's largest inland freshwater fisheries in the lower basin, which represents a critical food and protein source for the poor. It would be very costly if at all possible to replace this through agricultural expansion or import let alone the fact that currently the fishery is largely on a subsistence basis.

An often critical downstream impact of upstream infrastructure for irrigation and hydropower is that upstream dams may starve downstream reaches and coasts, e.g. the "sediment and nutrient trap" in the Nile, Indus, Mississippi and Mekong Basin. This may lead to deltas eroding, loss of nutrients and downstream agricultural and aquaculture production, and loss, or even collapse of coastal fisheries.

Preserving natural capital and ecosystem services while satisfying growing demands for water for food and energy production is a challenge faced by most trans-boundary basins in the South, such as loss of natural flooding in the Senegal and Lake Chad Basins that have led to losses of ecosystem services and production. In many such basins, needs have arisen to restore natural flooding, or to retrofit infrastructure to mitigate impacts. The lesson is that immediate action in the planning stage clearly is preferable to damage control at a very high cost later.

The victims of water-food-energy insecurity are the poorest. Seventy per cent of populations in international basins in the South are poor, e.g., in the Niger, Congo and Mekong Basins, and ecosystem-based livelihoods for the poor need to be protected. In the Mekong, 30 per cent of the population living less than 15 km from the river depend on water-related income.

Some Key Messages for Hydro-diplomacy

The challenges addressed above, including many examples from trans-boundary basins worldwide, lead to some key messages for hydro-diplomacy if we are to achieve water, energy and food security in trans-boundary basins.

Firstly, satisfying growing demands for water, food and energy, while maintaining a healthy environment, can only be addressed in cooperation, moving "outside our boxes" and talking together across sectors and stakeholder groups in public-private-civic partnerships.

Secondly, the water, energy and food security nexus calls for new thinking in shared basins, combining multiple demands and uses. This requires reconciling national and regional interests in efforts to making the total more than the sum of the parts, and thus enhancing regional stability.

Thirdly, achieving water, energy and food security in trans-boundary basins calls for regional agreements backed by national policies and actions. This can only be achieved by adopting the basin approach, and empowering basin management entities to assist national decision-making.

Fourthly, the livelihoods of the poor, and our natural capital and biodiversity, are essential assets that we cannot afford to lose. We need to adopt an ecosystems approach to IWRM and nexus thinking.

And fifthly, trans-boundary cooperation towards water, energy and food security must be scientifically based, and convey legitimate and understandable messages to decision-makers. We need to improve the science-policy dialogue through decision support systems based on shared data and information, building trust in the process.

✧

COSTS
BENEFITS

HYDRO ETHICS
HYDRO PHILOSOPHY
HYDRO CALLOUSNESS
HYDRO INTELLIGENCE
HYDRO COMMON SENSE
HYDRO RIGHTS
HYDRO POLITICS
HYDRO SOCIOLOGY
HYDRO COMPETITION
HYDRO SOLIDARITY
HYDRO DIPLOMACY
HYDRO PERSUASION
HYDRO LOGIC

SHARING WATER ACROSS BORDERS

Water and Diplomacy

C.M. Shafi Sami

MOTHER NATURE has endowed us with an enormous amount of water. Water covers three quarter of earth's surface. But an overwhelming 97 per cent of the total quantity of water lies in the seas as saline water and more than 2 per cent in the form of ice and snow; thus 99 per cent of this vast endowment is still beyond easy reach of mankind and beyond its ability to harness. Maximum availability of fresh water to meet human needs is thus no more than a bare 1 per cent of this vast amount.

In the past, this small availability was plentiful to meet the basic needs of mankind and abundant for its survival. But as population grows it creates additional demand for fresh water to meet mankind's basic needs like food production, agriculture, pisciculture, horticulture and irrigation. As quality of life improves new needs are created and the demands on fresh water increases to respond to those emerging needs. Advancement of civilisation constantly generates a whole new set of demands of enormous magnitude and varied character. Vital to a nation's survival and prosperity involving the entire gamut of economy, this is a resource that has no substitute. It is no paradox then that despite the vastness of quantity of water, fresh water availability is progressively diminishing and water is increasingly being seen as a scare resource.

Experts apprehend that in not too distant future almost half of world population will come under severe threat of water scarcity. Many ecosystems will be unable to cope with the rapidly growing demands of the basic needs, improvement of quality of life and economic development of an ever increasing world population. As scarcity accentuates balancing the competing needs of societies will become a contentious issue between regions within many countries of the world. It will be an even more formidable task in case of international or trans-boundary water resources which are shared by two or more states. The enormity of the task can better be appreciated when we realise that there are 263 trans-boundary water sources in the world that straddle or cross political boundaries of one or more sovereign states, constituting over 80 per cent of worlds fresh water sources—rivers and aquifers. Most of the water basins are shared by just two countries; others are shared by three or more countries—with the Danube River being shared by as many as 18 nations. As many as 145 countries of the world have territories within one or more trans-boundary water sources. More than 95 per cent of the territories of as many as 33 countries lie within international river basins making them totally dependent on shared water resources. Trans-boundary water resources cover about half of the land surface of the earth and as much as 40 to 50 per cent of the total world population is dependent on shared water resources.

Some experts believe that water scarcity has all the potential of becoming a source of international conflict. After the conclusion of peace treaty with Israel, President Anwar Sadat of Egypt said: "The only matter that could take Egypt to war again is water." A decade later that country's Foreign Minister prognosticated that "the next war in the Middle East would be fought over the waters of the Nile, not politics." Ismail Serageldin of the World Bank gave a warning in late last century that, "If the wars of this century were fought over oil, the wars of the next century will be fought over water—unless we change our approach to managing this precious and vital resource." Many statesmen and observers believe that trans-boundary character of water sources combined with population pressures, competing national interests and increased water scarcity will lead to intense inter-state conflicts. There are many experts who predict that these conflicts will escalate to 'water wars' in the future threatening regional and international stability.

On the other hand, there is a strong belief that rather than causing open conflict, trans-boundary water can serve as stimulus for cooperation. The need of water together with the prospect of sharing benefits from equitable use of these common water resources for sustainable socioeconomic development provides incentives for trans-boundary inter-state cooperation. According to the Food and Agricultural Organization (FAO), over the last millennium more than 3,600 treaties on international water resources have been negotiated with more than 200 such treaties being signed during the last century alone. As against that, last century saw no more than only 37 acute disputes involving violence. History also testifies that seldom has water been the sole cause of a violent conflict. On the contrary water use and sharing agreements have been successfully negotiated even in conditions of inter-state hostility over other issues. A declared state of hostility between Jordan and Israel did not prevent them from negotiating and cooperating on water related matters. In South East Asia Cambodia, Thailand, Viet Nam and Laos have cooperated on water sector under the purview of Mekong River Commission, the Viet Nam War notwithstanding. Belying the dire predictions of 'water wars' the Nile riparian states are now seeking to develop the river in a cooperative manner, sharing substantial socio-economic benefits, and promoting regional peace and security. Another significant aspect of cooperation in water sector is that once cooperation is forged the benefits of cooperation ensure that it becomes enduring and resilient. Nations deriving benefit from water treaties find it prudent to hold on to them and continue to draw its advantage. The most remarkable resilience has been demonstrated by the Indus Water Treaty signed in 1960 between India and Pakistan; it survived more than half a century's bitter hostility between the neighbours and withstood two bitterly fought wars between them.

For long the international community has deliberated on various theoretical approaches governing the utilisation, share, management and quality control of the shared water resources. These have resulted in the formulation of four major doctrines over a period of time. The main characteristics of these are presented in easily understood simple terms. The Doctrine of Absolute Territorial Sovereignty was propounded in 1885 by US Attorney General J. Harmon and is popularly known as Harmon Doctrine. It gave all riparian states full and unlimited rights to whatever it wished to do with the water course falling within its territory without any regard for the needs and concern of other riparian countries. In reality, this doctrine gave exceedingly favourable dispensation to an upper riparian state; a country having absolute sovereignty over the portion of an international watercourse within its borders would be free to use or divert all of the water from an international watercourse, leaving none for downstream states. This doctrine was invoked by the US on the flows of the Rio Grande river as an upper riparian state vis-à-vis Mexico. Interestingly, US itself rejected this doctrine in 1950 during its dispute over the waters of Columbia River in which Canada was the upper riparian state with US lying down stream. On the other extreme and diametrically opposed to the Harmon Doctrine is the Doctrine of Absolute Territorial Integrity which asserts that a lower riparian country has the right to demand uninterrupted natural flow of water from the territory of any upper riparian state. This doctrine held that an upstream state could do nothing to interfere with the natural flow of the river into a downstream state. The third doctrine that deserves mention is the Doctrine of Limited (Restricted) Territorial Sovereignty which seeks to strike a reasonable balance between the earlier two doctrines. This doctrine gives recognition of a state's sovereignty over the water resources in its territory but enunciates that all states have equal sovereignty over the common water resources and hence sovereignty of one state is not unfettered and is 'limited' by the sovereignty of another state. Simply put every state has the sovereign right to use waters lying within its territory provided its use does not prejudice the sovereign rights and uses of another state sharing the common watercourse. This doctrine guarantees reasonable water to all co-riparian states under reasonable conditions; the doctrine seeks to espouse the principle of equitable utilisation and no harm done to other riparian states. The fourth doctrine is known as the Doctrine of Community of Co-riparian States or Community of Interests. It is an attempt to improve upon the concepts in the doctrine of limited sovereignty. It enunciates a common legal right of all co-riparian states on international water resources. The doctrine establishes a perfect equality of all riparian states in the use of entire water course and excludes any preferential privilege for any riparian state in relation to others.

Serious attempts at formulating international laws on water began in the early last century. Since then, international community, by and large, has tried to provide a framework and general guidelines. In the process, some norms and principles regulating the governance of trans-boundary water resources have evolved and gained general acceptance. These are mostly derived from the many treaties concluded between nations, judicial decisions at international level and recommendations of advisory bodies, private organisations as well as studies by water experts. There is now an explicit recognition that all riparian states are entitled to the use of international water course in an equitable and reasonable manner. Another important principle has now achieved international recognition that riparian states have an obligation not to cause significant harm to the other riparian states and all riparian states shall exercise due diligence in the utilisation of international water resources. Although these principles have generated interminable debates on how exactly to determine reasonableness, equity, significant harm and due diligence, these concepts are indeed important milestones in achieving good governance of international water courses. Some of these norms and principles are contained in the 1966 Helsinki Rules on the Uses of the Waters of International Rivers and the 1997 UN Convention on Non-navigational Uses of International Water Courses.

The 1997 UN Convention represents an important step towards the strengthening of the rule of law in international waters. Of particular importance is the principle embodied in this Convention requiring a state to utilise the watercourse, in its territory, in a manner that is equitable and reasonable vis-à-vis the other states sharing that water course. Another crucially important provision is the obligation imposed on a state not to cause any significant harm to other states sharing an international water course. The Convention also puts an obligation on a state undertaking any project to notify other states of planned activities to allow the other states to assess if there would be any significant adverse effects; the intention is to obviate such adverse effects. These are very positive and important principles which will promote good governance in this increasingly critical area of international relations. The Convention will be the only treaty governing shared freshwater resources of universal applicability, once it comes in to force. When and if it comes into force its influence is likely to grow.

Conflict or cooperation on international waters—clearly there are two contradictory and clashing prognoses before us. Whether it is averting the threat of conflict or harnessing the prospects of cooperation, the challenge before the world is formidable. The quality of governance of trans-boundary waters will play a role of paramount importance in determining which of these two courses mankind will opt for. As decisions relating to utilisation, share, management and quality control of the international water fall within the jurisdictions of more than one country, the governance encompassing these elements will bring into play inter-state interactions. Diplomacy, the medium of inter-state interactions, has a pivotal role in balancing the competing interests of states. One also has to reckon that the dynamics of water negotiations is in a state of flux as it moves from zero-sum attitudes to positive-sum integrative win-win approaches, from right based volumetric sharing to the creation and sharing of benefits derived from water resources. This development will create more economic opportunities and simultaneously bring into play additional political challenges. Synthesising and harmonising the complex mix of economic opportunities and political challenges will thus impose pronounced demands on diplomacy.

The complexity of the inter-state interactions is further compounded by the fact that the international laws on trans-boundary water resources are poorly developed and some of the norms and principles developed are open to varying interpretations and yet others are even contradictory. Additionally the 1997 UN Convention, achieved after painstaking efforts of more than two decades, has yet to come into force as it falls short of the requisite number of ratifications, even after one and half decade after its adoption. Another worrying aspect is that international water regime lacks international institutional mechanism to enforce agreed upon norms, principles and laws as much as it lacks conflict resolution mechanisms in case a dispute erupts. Like many other international laws, trans-boundary water resources laws are thus not easily enforceable. In the absence of international enforcement mechanism and in view of their generalised nature these principles and laws are not legally binding. There is a growing feeling among experts that these principles and laws need to be more concrete and precise. Simultaneously with harmonising inter-state interests, in clearer and unambiguous terms it will be of vital importance to concretise and crystallise principles and laws relating to the regimes of these precious resources and to create institutional mechanism that will have the capacity of enforcement as well as conflict resolution. On all these counts diplomacy will be called upon to play a role of crucial and overwhelming importance in the days ahead.

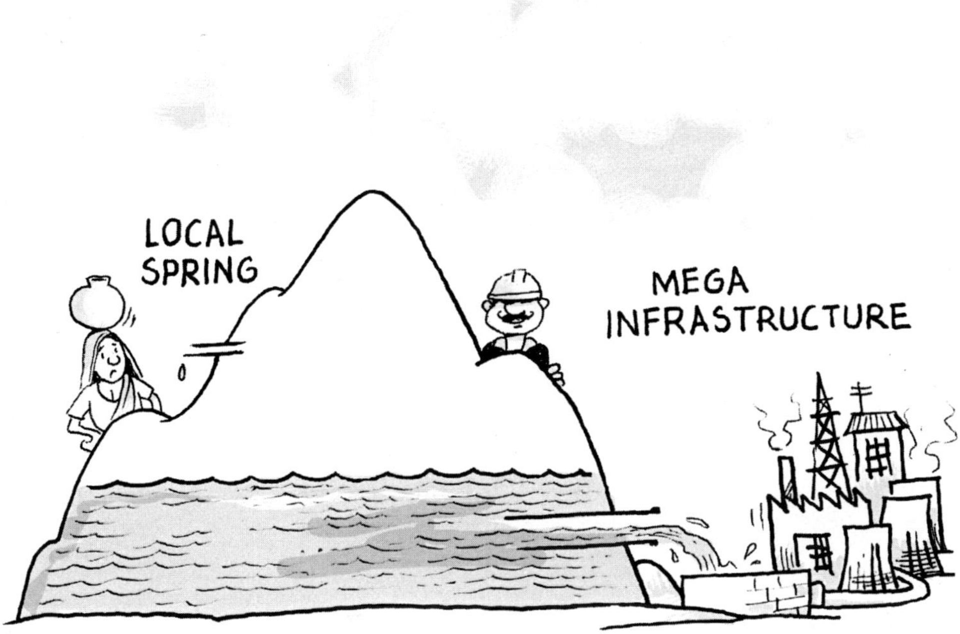
LOCAL
SPRING
MEGA
INFRASTRUCTURE

HYDRO ETHICS
HYDRO PHILOSOPHY
HYDRO CALLOUSNESS
HYDRO INTELLIGENCE
HYDRO COMMON SENSE
HYDRO RIGHTS
HYDRO POLITICS
HYDRO SOCIOLOGY
HYDRO COMPETITION
HYDRO SOLIDARITY
HYDRO DIPLOMACY
HYDRO PERSUASION
HYDRO LOGIC

SHARING WATER ACROSS BORDERS

Blue Diplomacy: Fostering Sustainable and Equitable Growth

Johan Gely

Switzerland has ideals for our planet, where peace, human rights, economic growth and environment play a key role. We strive to have a good record of solidarity and active peace efforts. Switzerland, the water tower of Europe, tries to be an exemplar up-stream country investing a lot to deliver good water quality and quantity to their neighbour countries and sometimes absorbing part of floods to avoid major disasters downstream. With its abundant water resources and responsible water management practices, we would like to believe that Switzerland is immune from global freshwater challenges. This is not the case!

With our high standard of living, the Swiss have a water footprint much larger than the world average. While we import products—in particular, food—that are water-intensive, our service-based exports are not. This means that 82 per cent of Switzerland's water footprint is made out of our country, and often in regions where water resources are scarcer than in ours.

This underlines the relevance of Switzerland's engagement and responsibility to contribute to resolving global water issues—and not just out of international solidarity, but also because our own development depends on it.

Switzerland is involved in a new type of cooperation which combines peace promotion and the sustainable management of water resources.

Freshwater is essential to all forms of life and fundamental for human health, sustainable growth, food security and ecosystem protection. At the beginning of the 3rdmillennium, water resources felt direct impacts of rapid global changes caused by population growth, migration, urbanisation, climate change, land-use changes and economic development among others.

Many countries in the world are facing serious water shortage or climate-induced flooding which increase competition for access, thus explaining why it is becoming the most pressing environmental and social issue of the 21st century. From this point of view, many trans-boundary rivers are a hot spot justifying the Swiss Agency for Development and Cooperation's (SDC) engagement with its instrument of cooperation.

In that context, the Blue Peace framework launched in 2009 by Switzerland along with its partners has attracted interest in different parts of the world. It allows SDC to respond to explicit demands made by political leaders worldwide and to address the critical challenges of water security through the development of collaborative solutions for sustainable regional water management.

The diagnostic

It is a known fact that water is vital for life and for development. All sectors of the economy use water, directly or indirectly, as an input, a sink for wastewater, and also as part of the social and cultural fabric of communities and nations.

The global water crisis is multiform: By 2050, the world may have a population three times of what it was in 1950 and nine times of what it was in 1750. From 1950 to 2050, we would have lifted more than five billion people out of poverty. These developments are extremely positives. However, they will not be free of cost. The biggest price we will pay will be in terms of growing demand on water. With these figures in mind we all understand that the water crisis is quantitative.

It is also qualitative: More than 80 per cent of used water is discharged without any treatment. Water pollution of rivers, lakes, groundwater and oceans is on the rise. According to some estimates, at least two billion people use water that is unsafe. Two and a half billion people still have no access to proper sanitation, all this had implications for health, dignity and ultimately prosperity. Sanitation is therefore a fundamental part of water management. It reduces net availability of water substantially.

The bottom line being water issues are pressing. Water supply is unlikely to keep pace with water demand. Over 50 per cent of the global population may live under water stress by 2050.

The consequences of these mounting water challenges are multi-fold:

- They can have dramatic impacts on the quality of life of millions of individuals by exacerbating disease, hunger, and poverty.
- They can negatively affect regional and global food security.
- They can produce electricity gaps and hamper economic development, as many developing countries rely heavily on hydropower in their energy mix.
- They can also fuel social tensions and further weaken fragile states; and
- They can exacerbate regional tensions, particularly if water-sharing arrangements are absent, inadequate or insufficiently implemented.

At river basin levels, existing trans-boundary water management practices and arrangements have reached the limits of their effectiveness in several parts of the world. In almost every region, lower riparian countries claim historical rights (and therefore want to keep the status quo) to water resources while upper riparian countries claim territorial rights (and therefore renegotiation of volumetric allocations) to accrue access to water resources within their jurisdiction for agriculture, electricity generation and urbanisation, and therefore livelihoods, trade and economic development, human security and international relations.

In various places of the world, unless new arrangements are founded, the tension between riparian countries is expected to increase and can lead to wider political conflicts. It would not be confined to the neighbouring countries as third parties and multilateral organisations would be involved in the form of investments (historical and non-traditional financiers are competing in this endeavour although to increase their geopolitical gains) of hydraulic infrastructure development and land reclamation projects to help countries meet their national needs.

As many regions were not developed for several centuries leaving the flow of watercourses undisturbed, with the development of new balances of power in river basin thanks to different economical, social and political dynamics and trends, trans-boundary water conflicts will be a new phenomenon to be witnessed in the 21st century.

Finally, at local level, water has often been used to cement political loyalties. It was a fundamental part of the social contract between citizen and state. Therefore water was provided for free, or subsidised. Hence, in many places, water's potential exhaustion threatens existing political balances.

To address competing demands and rights on water resources in the same basin, it is often necessary to consider high value trade-offs between water and other public goods such as transit rights, electricity and agriculture. Such trade-offs require substantial financial and security decisions requiring the involvement of all branches of the governments in addressing trans-boundary water issues from a security, economic, social, cultural and environmental perspectives. This approach should also include management practices that improve resilience to floods, droughts and other water-related disasters.

Water Diplomacy

Water resource management is more and more subject to significant pressure from political forces and will impact the way political relations and alliances are framed. In recent years, it has moved rapidly into the mainstream of international affairs and shaped the foreign policy of riparian countries in their mutual relationships. This is what is known as water diplomacy. In the future, the key geopolitical resources in many regions will be water much more so than sovereign access to fossil energy or food.

To confront this new type of security issue, we need a new type of solution. The response is not easy but there are many benefits of dealing with water challenges for human welfare, the economy and the environment. It is all about encouraging the emergence of a new type of diplomacy, the "blue diplomacy" with the objective of fostering sustainable and equitable growth.

Water is a solution for food security, for energy security, for human health, and for climate change adaptation. It is also a solution for economic growth: it is estimated that more sustainable water practices could generate about $17 trillion of global GDP. Such practices could also decrease by 21 per cent the number of children suffering from malnourishment. Beyond the development agenda, water can be a vital source for cooperation. Joint water management, for example, can become an important confidence-building measure, helping to reduce tension in a wider conflict setting.

Our Engagement: The Blue Peace Initiatives

Switzerland believes that water is becoming a new common challenge, which is bringing people and governments together to find innovative solutions to water challenges. According to Switzerland experience, in Asia, policymakers are ready to discuss transparent, coherent and cost efficient set of policies, laws and institutional responsibilities, including regulation and compliance mechanism at the local, national and regional levels for sustainable (based upon sharing social, economical, environmental and political benefits) water resource management.

Principles at the forefront of the "Blue Peace" initiatives are built using two pillars and they are:

Pillar 1: Engaging a Blue Peace Network for Political Dialogues

The "Blue Peace" puts forward an innovative approach to engage political leaders—those political officials who have an overall responsibility for agriculture, economy, finance, education, health, foreign relations, security, technological developments and budgetary decisions, the public, the parliament, the civil society, the academic sector and the media in harnessing and managing collaborative solutions for sustainable regional and basin water management. It allows us to trade off issues related to regional water management in a broader perspective.

The network is a common space, an enabling environment for political dialogues and cooperative management structures, projects and treaties in key hot spots river basins (taking advantage, when possible, of existing international arrangement as for example the UN International Water Conventions).

It introduces a new form of collaboration based on mutual understanding between politicians, water experts, users and the people living in the basin, and creates new opportunities for improving trans-boundary cooperation with basin wide-learning and influencing. Capacity building activities to enhance common understanding of principles of governance and options for the local populations to become a strong voice to defend their interest in water management is an important subset of our activities.

It makes a path for the evolution of a regional political and diplomatic community in water and creates new opportunities for resolving protracted water related conflicts.

This network is engaged (through workshops, bilateral and multilateral talks, seminars, conferences, desks and fields studies), at the request of the riparian countries, in examining present and future water security issues in specifics river basins or regions. As a result of their work, the Blue Peace Network publishes a "Blue Peace Report" on ways to address the implementation of innovative short, medium and long term recommendations to catalyse improvements in water management.

This process, which can last until 18 months, is fundamental to create a momentum and foster trust as a sound basis of a good relationship to enhance negotiation and improve understanding of water sovereignty, sharing benefits perspectives and support trans-boundary governance reforms, in one word, to craft a new water future in the recipients region.

Pillar 2: Implementing Tangible Joint Strategic Operations to Sustain Political Dialogues

The actors of the Blue Peace Initiatives are then applying these recommendations through the implementation of joint, concrete, realistic, consensual and innovative activities, projects, methods, tools, approaches and initiatives to catalyse improvements in water management in targeted basins (in Asia, Africa and America). The practice of water diplomacy benefit from example from joint action associated with the development of viable hydrological modelling and water flows levels measurements (from on the ground or via remote sensors) essentials for informed decision-making. Hence we support, in various basins, the introduction of common standards for the quantification, management and exchange of water data. We contribute also to the development of trans-boundary master plans, legal frameworks and joint river management institutions with model character balancing the needs for agriculture, industry, households and ecosystems, and integration of the models into international policy dialogue.

The two pillars enable some concrete steps forward in water diplomacy. We use the results obtained at basin levels in existing (or when not existing by creating them) regional mechanisms/platforms of political dialogue to help political leaders (and the poor) base their management decision on viable water data information.

This is done with the mobilisation of the Blue Peace Network through various advocacy and communication modalities (speeches, articles and TV broadcast etc.) and in the form of informal or formal policy, political and diplomatic briefings and meetings during which support for enhanced water management are collectively expressed. By these means, the initiative intends to create a constituency for the principles and processes of the blue peace framework in selected regions.

Conclusion

Water is an astonishingly complex and subtle force shaping our future. In front of water crisis, "business as usual" water management will undermine human development, economic growth and national security in many regions of the world.

The global water crisis is one of the major challenges of this century, we have enough water worldwide to respond to this challenge but we need to mobilise the whole water sector of our society (public, private sector, research and, of course, civil society).

The blue peace initiative makes a path for the evolution of a regional political and diplomatic community in water and creates new opportunities for resolving protracted water related conflicts. We hope that it will serve another objective: to foster trust between stakeholders which can go beyond water issues and be the sound basis of a good relationship, preventing future or potential conflicts related to water management.

Tackling water risks is not just an imperative, but also an opportunity. Our opportunity is to lay the basis for a "water-secure" world today. A world in which our freshwater resources are managed in a sustainable manner, in which access to water is secured for people, food production, ecosystems, energy and industry; a world in which we are protected from pollution and water hazards. And a world in which water is a catalyst of cooperation rather than a source of conflict. As the "water castle" of Europe, through long lasting negotiations, Switzerland has gained solid technical, scientific and political expertise in water management and is using this expertise and its network to path the way for a "water-secure" world using the tools of its "Blue Diplomacy".

EVERYBODY LIVES DOWNSTREAM!

HYDRO ETHICS
HYDRO PHILOSOPHY
HYDRO CALLOUSNESS
HYDRO INTELLIGENCE
HYDRO COMMON SENSE
HYDRO RIGHTS
HYDRO POLITICS
HYDRO SOCIOLOGY
HYDRO COMPETITION
HYDRO SOLIDARITY
HYDRO DIPLOMACY
HYDRO PERSUASION
HYDRO LOGIC

SHARING WATER ACROSS BORDERS

Hydro-diplomacy: Putting Cooperative Investment at the Heart of Trans-boundary Water Negotiations

Olivier Cogels

A Context of Growing Investment Needs

It is well known that in the developing world, rapid population growth, rising standards of living, and climate change significantly increase the investment needs for energy production, domestic, industrial, and agricultural water supply, flood control, wastewater treatment, protection of ecosystems, navigation, mining, etc. Many governments consider that their rivers still offer a large untapped potential and that water infrastructure investments, especially for hydropower generation, will accelerate poverty alleviation and will boost economic growth. In Africa, less than 10 per cent of the hydropower potential is exploited and in most developing countries, water storage per capita is still one order of magnitude lower than in industrialised countries. It is thus not surprising that in several parts of the world, water infrastructure projects are mushrooming, exerting high pressure on the increasingly scarce and fragile water resources.

On the financial front, new investors, such as China, India, Brazil, Malaysia and South Korea, are gaining leadership in the water resources development arena. In Africa, over the past 10 years, China alone invested more in hydropower than all conventional development banks combined, including the World Bank, the African Development Bank and the Islamic Development Bank.

A Complex Hydro-diplomatic Challenge

Most countries in the world share their rivers with one or more of their neighbours. And because water does not recognise political boundaries, water infrastructures such as large dams and water diversions inevitably generate trans-boundary impact, at the risk of severing geopolitical disputes. Preventing this poses a complex hydro-diplomatic challenge. The main obstacles are lack of trust between countries and national sovereignty issues. Governments and their public opinions thus need convincing arguments about the political, socioeconomic and environmental benefits of stronger trans-boundary cooperation agreements and institutions.

Fortunately, good arguments are not lacking, among which the moral obligation of preventing conflicts is the most obvious one. There are various theories about the risks of water wars, ranging from rather optimistic to very pessimistic. Geopolitical tensions relating to the Jordan, the Blue Nile, the Aral Sea, the Tigris and the Euphrates, are well known. Tensions are also emerging in several other international river basins. Although it is difficult to assess the risks of armed inter-state conflicts, it is undeniable that lack of cooperation already leads to political crises and to loss of human lives and of billions of dollars.

There are also other good reasons to strengthen trans-boundary cooperation. Protecting downstream countries against floods and chemical disasters is one of the most relevant. Investment optimisation is another one. Indeed, there are topographical and climatic factors that make coordinated development and management of irrigation, hydropower and navigation at basin scale much more cost effective. In addition, in a context of increasing water scarcity, more countries will not be able to achieve food self-sufficiency and will thus increasingly depend on regional integration and food trade. Finally, the co-financing of large infrastructures in a regional context, especially in the energy sector, offers significant commercial advantages.

Hydro-diplomatic Instruments and Platforms

Since the end of World War II, hydro-diplomacy has enabled the negotiation of several bilateral and multilateral treaties and the establishment of related basin institutions and organisations. However, there are still a number of major international watercourses which are not yet equipped with such diplomatic instruments. Furthermore, most of the existing basin organisations face serious financial difficulties and are largely dependent on external funding. Only a few rely significantly on financial resources generated by jointly owned infrastructure.

The 1997 UN Convention on the Law of the Non-navigational Uses of International Watercourses, ratified by only 30 countries, has not yet entered into force. However, its key principles—equitable utilisation, duty to take measures to prevent harm and duty to cooperate—are now widely accepted as customary international law. And although these principles leave the door open to much interpretation, they at least provide a useful framework for the negotiation of more specific agreements. Likewise, the UNECE Water Convention provides useful legal guidance on reasonable and equitable use of trans-boundary waters.

Hydro-diplomacy involves a wide range of stakeholders. Although the leading role is usually played by water departments, negotiations also involve ministries of foreign affairs, economy and finance, Planning, and of other sectors. Heads of State are involved whenever deemed necessary. Parliamentarians, civil society, donors, development banks, regional economic communities, etc., are also increasingly influential.

Many basin organisations have well-established policy dialogue mechanisms, e.g., a Joint Technical Committee, a Council of Ministers and a Summit of Heads of State. Dialogue mechanisms at basin level and at country level also allow formal and informal discussions between governments and donors. Dialogue platforms also appear at regional and global levels. All these hydro-diplomatic platforms offer opportunities to governments and other stakeholders for exerting influence on the priorities and strategic orientations of trans-boundary cooperation agreements and institutions.

Shift in the Strategic Orientation of Donor Support

Development aid is an important dimension of international relations and is often used as a leverage to influence the role and priorities of organisations.

Over time, the priorities of the donor community regarding trans-boundary water cooperation have shifted. In the early days, the focus was clearly on joint planning, financing, building and operation of large dams. A well-known political success story is the joint financing, implementation, and operation of the Manantali and Diama dams on the Senegal River within the scope of the OMVS[1] programme for integrated development of irrigation, hydropower and navigation.

Due to growing environmental concerns and strong controversies about water infrastructures, the international community is today less willing to put the emphasis on the investment facilitation and coordination role of basin institutions. Donor support tends to be more and more oriented toward water governance and environmental protection issues. Few bilateral donors accept to finance the preparation of infrastructure projects. Hydro-diplomacy tends to be more environmentally than economic.ally oriented.

The case of the Mekong River Commission (MRC) is an interesting example of this shift. Half a century ago, agreeing on joint basin development plans was the main focus of the Mekong Committee (1957-1977) and of the Interim Mekong Committee (1978-1989). But since the signing of the "Mekong Agreement" in 1995, donors have oriented MRC's activities mainly toward information and knowledge management, while downplaying its investment facilitation role. This is clearly illustrated by the donor group statement made during the MRC Ministerial Council of December 2005: "Donors are concerned about the direction towards increased emphasis on MRC becoming an organization that drives investments. In our view, the MRC should maintain and strengthen its unique role as a knowledge-based river basin organization to support decisions on developments in the basin. MRC's knowledge base has wide applications. However, the investment facilitation role should be limited to screening of projects based on MRC's knowledge and expertise and not undertake pre-feasibility studies."

---

[1] Organisation pour la Mise en Valeur du Fleuve Sénégal, established in 1972 by Mali, Mauritania and Senegal.

With such a vision of the role of basin organisations, there is a risk that they will continue to be excluded from the national investment planning process. Governments will continue to complain about the lack of tangible results for the direct benefit of the population. They will also remain reluctant to increase their financial contributions. Basin organisations may well get stuck in an endless trust building process, focusing mainly on knowledge management, thematic studies, environmental monitoring, etc., but playing an insignificant role in the negotiations about the most critical issues. No doubt that knowledge is essential for informed decision-making, but its generation and communication should first and above all be developed at national level, on the basis of the subsidiarity principle.

Promoting a "Doctrine of Cooperative Investment"

In many international river basins, it is the investment in water infrastructures which constitutes the main source of geopolitical tensions. An option, advocated by some stakeholders, is to try to stop or at least seriously slow down this type of investment. But in the current macro-economic context, this approach does not seem very realistic. Because such investments will probably continue at an accelerated pace, geopolitical tensions will inevitably arise if stronger cooperation between basin countries is not developed in the short term.

We believe that in order to help developing countries improve their water security, while pursuing peacefully and equitably their economic growth, hydro-diplomacy should put more emphasis on joint planning, financing and operation of water infrastructure investments, based on cost and benefit sharing. However, we think it would not be effective to negotiate agreements on individual projects in a piecemeal approach. Basin countries should negotiate the content of a "joint multi-sector investment programme" at the basin scale; a programme to be agreed upon at the highest political level.

The term "multi-sector investment programme" is understood here as "a well-balanced multi-sector portfolio of investment projects, supported by a coherent strategy, aiming to achieve a common goal." The term "investment" is used in its broad sense, including not only water infrastructures, but also environmental investments, information and monitoring systems, legal frameworks, and accompanying measures. The sectors include hydropower, irrigation, navigation, flood control, fisheries, environment and tourism. It is in the scope of such a "smart" joint programme that trade-offs and compensations can be negotiated and that the necessary social and environmental protection measures can be implemented. An example is the joint investment programme signed in 2008 by the nine Heads of States of the countries sharing the Niger River.

Cooperative investment planning may start with a basin-wide multi-sector investment opportunities analysis (MSIOA), such as achieved in 2009 by the World Bank for the Zambezi Basin. The joint programme requires regular updating within the scope of a participatory planning process (rolling plan), at the level of each sector separately as well as across sectors. It also needs the improvement and harmonisation of the legal framework.

We propose to call "doctrine of cooperative investment", the ideas and principles according to which trans-boundary water conflicts can be prevented if all major water infrastructure investments are part of a joint multi-sector investment programme at the basin scale, agreed upon at the highest political level. For most international river basins in the developing world, we believe that this doctrine should beat at the heart of hydro-diplomacy.

Need for Effective Organisational Structures

Planning and implementation of a joint multi-sector investment programme should be the primary role or "core business" of an effective organisational structure with adequate staffing and planning tools.

Usually, an international water treaty covers the aspects of water resources development, water governance and environmental protection. The same basin organisation is usually mandated with a too long list of "core functions", including data collection, knowledge management, planning, modelling, monitoring, pollution control, flood control, preparation of rules and procedures, resources mobilisation, etc. The investment related functions are drowned in a multitude of other functions, leading to haziness and lack of visibility.

One option would be the creation of new specialised organisations. Another option would be the restructuring of existing basin organisations in two separate entities—one supporting joint investment planning and coordination and one supporting water governance and environment protection. These two roles are indeed essential, but not compatible enough. Lessons can be drawn from the Nile Basin Initiative, in which the sub-basin organisations[2] focus on investment, while a basin-wide Nile-Secretariat puts the emphasis on governance.

On the basis of a better demarcation of roles, environmental monitoring and regulation would be performed more independently. Objective assessment of the individual and cumulative impacts of the investment programme would thus be possible, ensuring that each investment project is compliant with the principles agreed upon by the member states.

The investment support entity should be able to acquire leadership as a specialised regional organisation, playing a leading role in regional economic integration. Its financial resources should partly be generated by membership contributions and partly by the services provided, including the operation of infrastructures.

---

[2] The Eastern Nile Technical Regional Office (ENTRO) in Addis Ababa is implementing the Eastern Nile Subsidiary Action Program (ENSAP), while the Nile Equatorial Lakes Subsidiary Action Program (NELSAP) is implemented by a programme coordination unit (NELSAP-CU) in Kigali.

Conclusion

It is undeniable that in the developing world, water infrastructure investments will continue to occur at an accelerated pace. Without stronger investment cooperation at the basin scale, the world will face growing risks of serious geopolitical disputes and highly unefficient use of its scarce water resources. We therefore propose to put at the heart of hydro-diplomacy a "doctrine of cooperative investment", according to which trans-boundary water conflicts can be prevented if the main water infrastructure investments are part of a *"joint multi-sector investment programme"*, agreed upon at the highest political level. This requires proactive economic hydro-diplomacy, supported by appropriate organisational structures.

We are well aware that there is no one size fits all solution and that each basin has its own specificities in terms of climate, political context, development stage, etc, But we hope that the ideas developed here will provide food for thought for the political leaders and other stakeholders involved in hydro-diplomacy in various parts of the world.

HYDRO ETHICS
HYDRO PHILOSOPHY
HYDRO CALLOUSNESS
HYDRO INTELLIGENCE
HYDRO COMMON SENSE
HYDRO RIGHTS
HYDRO POLITICS
HYDRO SOCIOLOGY
HYDRO COMPETITION
HYDRO SOLIDARITY
HYDRO DIPLOMACY
HYDRO PERSUASION
HYDRO LOGIC

SHARING WATER
ACROSS BORDERS

Hydro-diplomacy for Hydro-harmony

Ramaswamy R. Iyer

LET ME begin with three points about the term 'hydro-diplomacy'. First, so far as I know, there is no special category of diplomacy called 'hydro-diplomacy'. Diplomacy is diplomacy, whether it relates to border disputes or water-related disputes or trade-related questions or any other issue between two countries. Secondly, 'hydro-diplomacy' is an ambiguous term; it could mean: (1) diplomacy devoted to water-related issues, or (2) diplomacy using water as a counter or an instrument. Our interest is clearly in the former. Thirdly, the connotation of the word 'diplomacy' is not entirely positive; it carries a suggestion of clever persuasion or manipulation for dubious ends. We want good diplomacy and not bad diplomacy.

Granting the need for diplomacy for resolving disputes between countries (or between States in a federal set-up) over trans-boundary rivers;, let us consider the issues that arise in that context. These could include riparian contestation, i.e., conflicting claims over the waters of the river between the upper and lower riparians; the phenomenon of 'lower riparian anxiety'; security concerns; concerns about the environmental impacts of upper riparian (or sometimes lower riparian) action or plans; and so on. The negotiations might be affected by strong feelings at the popular level and/or the politicisation of the issue in either country (or State). All these have figured in my own experience of water-related negotiations. In what follows I shall be drawing upon my Indian experience, but I hope that what I say will have some relevance beyond that context.

Before proceeding to my Indian experience, let me consider briefly what is needed to make river-water-related negotiations or hydro-diplomacy successful. First, the hydro-diplomat or negotiator must have a thorough and deep knowledge of the subject. This is not always the case in India. The briefing of a negotiator must be comprehensive, and must cover every issue that is likely to arise in the negotiations. This is of course true of all negotiations, but disputes over river waters tend to have a particularly complex and chequered history. Secondly, thorough and comprehensive preparations for negotiations presume the availability of all necessary data and information, which again is not always the case in India. The necessary data are sometimes not readily available, and sometimes simply do not exist. Quite often the diplomat has to manage with inadequate or fuzzy information. This is a deficiency that needs urgent attention.

Thirdly, the Government's brief to the negotiator must be very clear: it must spell out the objective precisely and fully, and must also define the flexibility given to the negotiator and its limits. Fourthly, there must be full internal consensus on the negotiating brief, secured through proper inter-ministerial, inter-agency, and Centre-State consultations, so as to avoid the possibility of different Ministries or agencies or Governments speaking in different voices. Finally, every effort must be made to ensure in advance that the outcome of the negotiations would be fully acceptable within the country not only at the governmental and political levels but also at the popular level. All these are elementary and obvious observations; it is unfortunate that it is necessary to state them.

Formal negotiations take place at the official level but it is necessary to create a positive ambience in both of the countries (or States) for a settlement of the dispute and for good relations at the people-to-people level. Non-official initiatives in this regard (known as Track II) are very useful. Track II talks must contribute to the success of Track I diplomacy. There must be a constant interaction between Track I and Track II. The role of Track II can be not merely facilitating and supplementary but also gap-filling and bridge-building when Track I talks are caught in a logjam because of rigid positions.

There are quite a few Track II initiatives in the context of India's relations with her neighbours. Within India, there has been a good Track II initiative in the Cauvery Dispute which has brought the farmers of the two main disputing States (Tamil Nadu and Karnataka) together in what is known as 'Cauvery Family' and promoted goodwill and understanding.

Let me proceed now to the issues that arise.

Taking water-sharing first, the Indus Waters Treaty 1960 became necessary because the line of partition in 1947 cut across the Indus system, and was the result of prolonged negotiations between the two new countries created by Partition, with the World Bank as mediator. It allocates the three eastern rivers, i.e., Ravi, Beas and Sutlej, to India, and the three western rivers, i.e., Jhelum, Chenab and Indus itself, to Pakistan, allowing some limited use of the western rivers by India subject to certain conditions. The Treaty was a final settlement of the water-sharing dispute between the two countries. It has managed to survive four wars. In that sense it must be regarded as a success. There is indeed some dissatisfaction in both countries with the water allocations under the Treaty. However, when a Treaty is negotiated over 10 years and is approved and signed at the highest levels, it must be presumed that it was the best outcome that was possible under the given circumstances. The operation of the Treaty has no doubt been characterised by persistent differences between the two countries, but they are not about water-sharing. I shall return to those differences later.

The Ganges Treaty, which resolved the protracted Ganga waters issue between India and Bangladesh, is essentially about sharing the waters of the Ganga in the lean season, i.e., from 1 January to 31 May each year, when the flows in the Ganga steadily decline, reaching the lowest level in the period from March to May, after which they begin to increase with the melting of the snows. The sharing point is Farakka. It will be recalled that the building of the Farakka Barrage by India was the starting point of the dispute. The sharing pattern is illustrated in the Treaty by a table divided into 10-day periods. The actual sharing at Farakka is watched by a joint India-Bangladesh team.

In so far as the Mahakali Treaty with Nepal is concerned, there is certainly a water-sharing aspect to it but it is mainly about the intended joint planning and implementation of the Pancheswar Project. The Treaty also contains some provisions meant to respond to certain longstanding concerns of Nepal arising from a history of chequered relations. Unfortunately, a combination of circumstances has virtually made the Treaty a dead letter. I shall not go into that story because it is not so much a story of hydro-diplomacy as one of a peculiarly difficult and complex relationship between India and Nepal. It is a relationship that is sui generis but it falls outside the purview of this paper. A common feature of water-sharing Treaties or agreements is an allocation or apportionment of waters, i.e., a segmentation of an integrated system. The Indus Waters Treaty carried out a drastic surgery on the Indus system, cutting it into two parts and allocating them to Pakistan and India respectively. The Ganges Treaty did not go quite so far, but it too apportioned Ganga waters at Farakka to India and Bangladesh. While any agreement is better than discord, such segmentation is clearly a non-ideal way of dealing with systems that are integral unities, hydrologically speaking. As a second best solution this may be acceptable, but it involves a limited view of a river as no more than the water that flows. This happens within a country also, in inter-State agreements or adjudication. This ignores hydrology and ecology.

It may be mentioned in passing that even the Helsinki Rules of 1966 and the more recent UN Convention on the Non-Navigational uses of International Watercourses of 1997(which has not received the required number of ratifications so far) are implicitly based on what I have referred to as an approach of segmentation.

Incidentally, it is interesting to note that most water-related conflicts arise from a major intervention in a river. So long as a river is flowing naturally with no significant human intervention in those natural flows, major conflicts do not arise between the upper riparian and the lower riparian. That situation changes dramatically as soon as a dam or a barrage is built on a river for storing or diverting its waters. Dams or barrages become the foci of conflicts because they change hydrology, geography, ecology, and power relations.

A further factor in such conflicts is the projection of an ever-increasing future water demand. The combined 'demands' of all the disputing countries on the waters of a river often exceed the flows in the river. Both India and Pakistan feel aggrieved over their respective shares in the Indus waters under the Treaty, but if both shares are to be enhanced, more water will be needed than is available in the river system. That observation applies also to the respective claims of India and Bangladesh on the lean season flows of the Ganga. Competitive unsustainable demand for water is at the heart of such disputes.

A still further factor is politics. Given the importance of water and the emotional attachment to the river, inter-country river water disputes inevitably have a political dimension. That by itself is not a bad thing, but when politics and nationalist fervour over-ride rationality, resolution becomes very difficult indeed. Farakka became an important element in Bangladeshi politics, and acquired a symbolic significance as representing everything that was wrong in India-Bangladesh relations. Similarly, the old Kosi and Gandak agreements came to symbolise everything that was wrong in India-Nepal relations.

There is a two-way relationship between water relations and political relations. There are periods during which water looms large and dominates the political relations between two countries. There are also periods when the overall political relationship influences the water relations. Both those statements can be illustrated from the history of India-Pakistan and India-Bangladesh relations.

From water-sharing let us proceed to another theme, namely lower riparian anxiety or insecurity. Lower riparian in general tend to worry about upper riparian actions and intentions. This anxiety could be about water security, i.e., worry about a vulnerable dependence on the upper riparian for the continued and reliable availability of water; or it could be about water and security, i.e., worry about the possible use of water by the upper riparian for hostile purposes; or it could be a combination of the two. Both these figure in the relations between Pakistan as the lower riparian and India as the upper riparian.

As the lower riparian on the Indus system, Pakistan tends to look with anxious eyes at any attempts by India to build structures on the western rivers. Structures give control, and Pakistan is reluctant to agree to India acquiring a measure of control over rivers that stand allocated to Pakistan. It is apprehensive of the structures in question enabling India either to reduce water-flows or to release stored waters and cause floods. Its objections are thus partly water-related and partly security-related. There are abundant safeguards for Pakistan in the Indus Waters Treaty, but despite those protective provisions Pakistan as a lower riparian has a visceral anxiety about Indian projects on the western rivers.

Bangladesh is the lowest riparian in the Ganga–Brahmaputra–Meghna system(s), and could understandably feel a certain sense of insecurity in relation to water, particularly considering the size of the immediate upper riparian, India, in terms of land and population. Bangladesh is very conscious of the fact that there are 54 rivers (including rivulets and streams) crossing the Indo-Bangladesh border, and that 94 per cent of the country's waters originate beyond its boundary. Clearly, it needs some reassurances regarding water. Fortunately, the most contentious (and at one time seemingly intractable) issue between India and Bangladesh, namely, the Ganga waters issue, which was a major component in the complex and difficult relationship between the two countries, stands resolved by the Ganges Water Sharing Treaty of 12 December 1996, which seems to have been working to the reasonable satisfaction of the two Governments. Agreements or treaties are needed on some of the other rivers (Teesta, Muhuri, Manu, Gumti, Khowai, Brahmaputra, Dharla and Dudh Kumar) that have been identified as important. Unfortunately a Treaty on the Teesta, which was expected to be signed when the Indian Prime Minister visited Dhaka in September 2011, has run into a political road block in India which shows no signs of disappearing so far.

Both India and Bangladesh are now experiencing what I have described as 'lower riparian anxiety' about reported possibilities of big Chinese projects on the Brahmaputra. China has stated that it is not planning any diversions of Brahmaputra waters, but this issue will undoubtedly figure prominently in future talks with China. The Indian anxiety in respect of the Brahmaputra is similar to the Pakistani anxiety in relation to Indian projects on the western rivers of the Indus system, but while Pakistan has the protection of the Indus Waters Treaty, India has no treaty with China on the Brahmaputra. This is an emerging issue which will continue to remain a factor in the political relations among India, Bangladesh and China in the foreseeable future.

Incidentally, at an international conference held at New Delhi in November 2011 on 'River Waters: Perspectives and Challenges for Asia', Prof Gabriel Lafitte, an Australian academic, made an important point which needs to be pondered. He pointed out that China, India, Bangladesh, and other countries think of the Tibetan plateau only as the source from which they get waters, and are not interested in the needs and concerns of the people who live there in harmony with nature and in a non-exploitative relationship with the permafrost.

Apart from water-sharing and security aspects, a further element in the context of trans-boundary rivers is the environmental impact of upper riparian action. Environmental impact assessments (EIAs) are of course standard requirements for all big projects, but EIAs may not always take trans-boundary impacts into account.

Bangladesh is worried about the adverse environmental and other impacts of India's gigantic project for the inter-linking of rivers. Even Nepal, an upper riparian, is worried about certain implications of the project. India has reassured them that the Himalayan rivers are not being touched for the time being, and that when that question arises Nepal and Bangladesh would be kept informed and their concerns taken into account. There has been a good deal of controversy regarding the project within India. A change of Government in 2004 had the effect of putting the project on hold much to the relief of its critics as well as neighbouring countries. Regrettably, the Supreme Court of India has complicated matters by re-activating the project through a direction to the Government of India to set up an Implementation Committee. However, we are not concerned with that story here.

Bangladesh has also been expressing concern about the environmental impact of the Tipaimukh project in India. The latest development in that story is that a joint committee of Indian and Bangladeshi experts is studying the matter.

A new factor that all countries must take into account is climate change and its likely effect on water resources. While the aspects that I have been discussing so far are apt to be divisive, one must hope that common concerns relating to climate change will bring the countries together in joint studies and joint or coordinated responsive action.

A river basin as a whole is a hydrological system and may itself be an ecological system, or part of a larger ecological system. For practical purposes it may be necessary to deal with the national segments of a river, or within a country with even smaller parts of the whole such as sub-basins or micro-watersheds, but any action or non-action in any part of the basin may have consequences elsewhere in the basin. It is not merely a question of interventions in the river or in surface run-off; there is also an interaction between groundwater and surface water. Reduction in river flows may affect the recharge of aquifers, and excessive extraction of groundwater may affect the base flow in the river. Ideally, therefore, everything that is done, whether it is a big project or groundwater drilling or local rainwater-harvesting or run-off capture, needs to be governed by a basin-wide or ecosystem-wide perspective. This means that all the countries in a river basin or ecosystem must come together in some institutional form to ensure that their separate or joint actions are governed by an overall perspective.

It will be noticed that I am not using the familiar terms 'bilateralism' and 'regionalism'. Those are political terms. I prefer to look at the matter from a holistic ecological perspective. Again, I have said that the countries concerned must come together in some institutional form, but have not specified a particular form such as a River Basin Organisation (RBO). If it is necessary to avoid segmentation and fragmentation, it is equally necessary to avoid excessive centralisation and bureaucratisation. The arrangements must not be such as to make national or local action very difficult or subject to serious delays. These are matters for negotiation among the countries concerned.

Broadly speaking, one can say that the RBO or whatever we call it must have a combination of political, professional, inter-disciplinary elements, must be fully representative of all categories of water-users, and must be fully and truly 'participatory'. It must be the apex of a nested set of institutions federating upwards from the watershed level to the basin (and inter-governmental) level. We do not need a top-down, bureaucratic, techno-centric monstrosity at the basin level.

The European Water Framework Directive mandatorily requires its sovereign member countries to do certain things. One does not know whether a multinational Ganga Commission or Brahmaputra Commission can be empowered to issue any such mandatory instructions to its member countries. It will be difficult enough to get concurrence in the very idea of a multinational body. The first step is to get all the countries to recognise the need for a system-wide harmonisation. A prerequisite for this is the will to cooperate. Once a basin-level institutional framework of the kind indicated above comes into being, one can hope that it will enhance cooperation over a period of time.

Finally, we also need harmony in a different sense. Riparian relations between countries are basically about rights: the respective rights of the lower riparian and the upper riparian. Rights are essentially a matter of contestation. We need to move not only from segmentation to holism but also from contestation to harmony. Hydro-diplomacy must lead to hydro-solidarity. This requires the rights perspective to be supplemented by a perspective of obligations: the mutual obligations of the lower and upper riparian. If I may invoke the old Indian word for this, I would say that the upper and the lower riparian must be mindful of their dharma towards one another. (The word dharma has many senses, but is being used here in that of duty or moral responsibility.) Rights are a necessary perspective but they divide; dharma unites and harmonises.

✧

HOME
WORK

HYDRO ETHICS
HYDRO PHILOSOPHY
HYDRO CALLOUSNESS
HYDRO INTELLIGENCE
HYDRO COMMON SENSE
HYDRO RIGHTS
HYDRO POLITICS
HYDRO SOCIOLOGY
HYDRO COMPETITION
HYDRO SOLIDARITY
HYDRO DIPLOMACY
HYDRO PERSUASION
HYDRO LOGIC

SHARING WATER ACROSS BORDERS

Hydro-Diplomacy: The Peace of Water

Loic Fauchon

"WATER IS LIFE", as we hear in all the languages of the world. "Everything was water", the Hindus say. "Water is 'wou-ki', the great uncertainty", write the Chinese. And in the Koran, one can read "God created all things from water".

At the source of all life, water is the universal symbol of fertility, purification and regeneration. Water is free. Water is the "Measure" or, according to others, the "Materia Prima", the most widespread yet vital substance.

Water is threatened—threatened of dependence when some intend to take ownership or divert it- threatened of spoilage when human inconsistency is at the origin of multiple forms of pollution- endangered when climate change increases drought episodes to the extreme. These threats are caused by humans and their erratic behaviours making mankind water's first enemy.

Demographic growth is proof of these threats. Every 10 years, the world population increases by one billion inhabitants. This new population establishes and concentrates mainly in megacities. Numbers of these great cities are parched with thirst or will be in the near future.

Economic, agricultural and industrial activity contributes to severely polluted the air and water. This other threat affects the health of billion of individuals. Pointing to the state of many rivers and groundwater resources, we can talk of "sanitary bombs" with slow burning fuses. But one day...

The climate adds to the difficulties we face because it seems to impose on us widening gaps between lack and excess of water. The impact is visible forcing us to overdesign certain infrastructures, sometimes to ensure access to an increasingly scarce water resource, and sometimes to protect ourselves against its overflows.

To this is often added the waste and poor management of water. Excessive consumption and watering, leaky pipes, inconsistent pricing sometimes represent another form of threat on the water resource.

Until now, humans have shown their inability to establish a new relationship to water that is fair and harmonious. Changing this relationship is a moral duty since it allows asserting that access to water is an essential right indispensable to the dignity of thousands of women and men.

Changing this relationship is also an economic necessity because without water, there can be no development, agriculture nor industry respectful of sustainable ecosystems and biodiversity.

Changing this relationship is a social imperative to keep turning back water-borne diseases which remain the principal cause of child mortality.

Changing this relationship means accepting to consume less and better manage the resource in a world of growing uncertainties where resources are increasingly scarce. And these uncertainties all lead to more tension which, without regulations, can lead to conflicts.

Water is concerned by the shift of the world from the West to the East and, to a lesser extent, from the North to the South. In India and China and in most of their neighbouring countries, the most difficult battles will be fought to guarantee the water resource, its distribution, usages and return to the natural environment.

The construction of infrastructures in all these emerging or developing countries will be essential to the survival of nearly half of humankind.

In this context, the need for water shifts towards places where guaranteed resources just don't follow.

Beyond the erratic behaviour of oil prices and energy in general, a protracted crisis is in sight for the poorest.

The consequences are immediate when it comes to access to water which has been increasingly depending on electricity supply during the last decades.

All this contributes to increase the crisis and tension factors since there is a close tie between water and stability. This is a huge responsibility for political and economical decision-makers.

This responsibility is even greater in the 260 or so trans-border catchments listed by the great geographer Aaron Wolf (Priscoli and Wolf, 2007) since they affect what is today most sensitive to human activity and relation to nature. Let's take three examples: first, that of food security with the demographic growth, rising standards of living, changing eating habits which increase the pressure on the use of the freshwater resources for riparian countries of a same river. We witness this with the Nile, Tigris or Niger rivers.

Then there are the soaring pollutions due to the emergence of those megacities which have delayed implementation of sewage treatment. This was the case in Europe until recently for the Rhine, Danube and Rhone rivers.

And lastly, the issue of floods and more generally water related disasters. Controlling floods, implementing catchment area policies, developing relations and hence cooperation on each bank of the rivers, these are challenges that concern several hundred million people.

Climate change with increased precipitation in some instances and severe drought episodes in others, will amplify these phenomena which, year after year, besides an unbearable human cost, devastates the economy of numerous States and destroys natural terrestrial and aquatic ecosystems

For simple and particularly sustainable solutions to be implemented rapidly at the scale of the contemporary world, the international community lacks the capacity to establish a dialogue and organise itself. Obviously, there is a need to develop the geopolitics of water and gradually impose real water diplomacy. This "hydro-diplomacy" must see to a better access balance in the great continental water reserves, to the resolution of potential trans-border conflicts and to the refinancing of the water and sanitation systems of the poorest countries.

In the future, we will have sufficient water if we accept to cooperate and share. Otherwise, we will continue to throw millions of human beings on the roads and oceans who will in turn bump against the walls and fences that the rich hastily erect. Avoiding tension and wars boils down to contributing to build water walls instead of walls of indifference. A "hydro-diplomacy" at the service of a shared coexistence strategy made up of sustainable development and more equitable sharing.

References

Delli Priscoli, Jerry and Aaron T. Wolf. (2007). *Managing Water Conflicts: Dispute Resolution, Public Participation, and Institutional Capacity-building.* Cambridge, UK: Cambridge University Press.

✧

TRESPASSERS WILL BE SHOT
SHOW YOUR IDENTITY
WELCOME!
WHO GOES THERE?
NO ENTRY
STOP
WATER AUTHORITY
BEWARE
Rustam

HYDRO ETHICS
HYDRO PHILOSOPHY
HYDRO CALLOUSNESS
HYDRO INTELLIGENCE
HYDRO COMMON SENSE
HYDRO RIGHTS
HYDRO POLITICS
HYDRO SOCIOLOGY
HYDRO COMPETITION
HYDRO SOLIDARITY
HYDRO DIPLOMACY
HYDRO PERSUASION
HYDRO LOGIC

SHARING WATER ACROSS BORDERS

Water Agenda at the OAS: An Example of 50 Years on Water Diplomacy in the Americas

Maximiliano Campos Ortiz

Introduction

In 1962 a request was made by the government of Ecuador to the General Secretariat of the Organization of American States (GS/OAS) for technical assistance in surveying and assessing Ecuador's natural resources and among the results there were the integrated reconnaissance and study of the natural resources of the Guayas River Basin on Ecuador's Pacific Coast. Since then and for more than 50 years the GS/OAS, has been supporting their member countries to develop plans, policies and projects oriented to improve management, protection, conservation and sustainable use of water resources while addressing other issues like poverty reduction. It is in this context that water resources become a factor for understanding, cooperation and integration, and at the same time is a mechanism that strengthens democracies, peace and promotes development; all of these have required an intensive diplomacy whose success depends on complementary instruments available.

Background scenario

America is a continent rich in water resources, approximately 25,000 km^3/year, and with an extraction rate of 3 per cent for domestic, industrial and agricultural use (Pacific Institute, 2011). The sub-region of Latin America and the Caribbean have one third of the renewable water resources of the world and, with only 15 per cent of the territory and 8.4 per cent of its population, receives almost 30 per cent of global precipitations (United Nations, 2010). Even with this considerable water capital, its continental distribution is largely heterogeneous and its availability is subject to numerous stressors, among them, water withdrawal for agriculture, mining, as well as deforestation and the destruction of basin catchments and recharge areas (United Nations, 2010). A lot of the water resources in the hemisphere are located along the borders, it is an underground and superficial transboundary resource (74 transboundary aquifers, ISARM-Americas Program, UNESCO-OAS, 2010-11), from which valuable political cooperation experiences have evolved, Cuenca del Plata Treaty (Argentina, Estado Plurinacional de Bolivia, Brazil, Paraguay, Uruguay), San Juan

Agreement on Guarani Aquifer (Argentina, Brazil, Paraguay, Uruguay). Even though these are very positive steps which sample important diplomatic efforts, much efforts still needs to include many other cases from North America, Central America and the Caribbean.

Still the Americas has 35 million people lacking of an improved source of water and more than 118 millions do not have access to basic sanitation (WHO and UNICEF 2012). Latin America and the Caribbean have made large progress fulfilling the Millennium Development Goals (MDGs) and it is possible that many countries will reach the potable water goal for 2015; however, it is also difficult that the sanitation goal could be accomplished in the same proportion. In the Americas, shortages and excesses in water resources are both recurrent problems which can also be associated to water diseases. Many of the climate change impacts are related to the variability in water resources in order to produce energy, provision of potable water, food, and in other productive sectors like industry and mining (CEPAL, 2010). At the same time, large amount of disasters are associated to water/climate, where climate change and climate variability are fundamentals in its exacerbation. There is also a limited vision on shared management of a transboundary water resources' approach in many parts of the Americas, even though this is a continent whose boundaries are demarcated by water bodies (rivers, lakes) and their shared basins accounts for more than 60 per cent of the territory.

During the first decade of the 21st century, multiple and simultaneous planetary crisis (finances, energy, climate, health, food) have been determinants of the capacity of many of the countries of the Americas to confront a water crisis characterised by:

- Exponential contamination of water bodies and decline in maintenance and restoration of hydraulic infrastructure for potable water, sanitation, hydroelectricity, transportation, tourism and recreation.
- Variations in water supply associated to climate variability and change.
- Increment in water demand due to population growth and associated services.

Besides remarkable efforts made in the Americas, the most common water scenario is still of weak institutions, fractured and/or obsolete legislation, limited financial mechanisms and public/private investments, non-articulated participation of civil society, private and academic sectors as well as government, and a strong need for a transparent action with access to information and accountability. It is evident then, that as in many other parts of the world, water crisis in the Americas is directly related to its governance, which is a fundamental element for integrated water resources management (IWRM) which at the same time represents a huge determinant to integral development, pacific coexistence and democracy.

The Organization of American States (OAS): A Platform for Water Diplomacy

The OAS is the oldest regional organisation in the world; it can be traced back to the Congress of Panama convened by Simón Bolivar in 1826. It was in 1889 that the First International Conference of American States was held in Washington,

D.C., with the objective of discussing and recommending for adoption, to their respective Governments, some plan of arbitration for the settlement of disagreements and disputes that may in future arise between them.[1] This Conference laid the foundations of what would later become the "Inter-American System" under which a set of institutions were gradually established to facilitate cooperation in specific areas, the Pan American Health Organization (1902), which later also became the regional office of the future World Health Organization; the Inter-American Juridical Committee (1906); the Inter-American Children's Institute (1927); the Inter-American Commission of Women (1928); the Pan American Institute of Geography and History (1928); the Inter-American Indian Institute (1940); the Inter-American Institute for Cooperation on Agriculture (1942); and the Inter-American Defense Board (1942), which were then followed by the Inter-American Development Bank, the Inter-American Commission on Human Rights, the Inter-American Court of Human Rights, the Inter-American Drug Abuse Control Commission, the Inter-American Telecommunication Commission, the Inter-American Committee on Ports, the Justice Studies Center of the Americas, and others.

The OAS as it is recognised actually came into being in 1948 with the signing in Bogotá, Colombia, of the Charter of the OAS, which entered into force in December 1951. The organisation was established in order to achieve among its member states, as stipulated in Article 1 of its Charter, "an order of peace and justice, to promote their solidarity, to strengthen their collaboration, and to defend their sovereignty, their territorial integrity, and their independence".

The Charter has been subsequently amended by a series of protocols during the period 1967-1997. The OAS brings together all 35 independent states of the Americas and constitutes the main political, juridical and social governmental forum in the Hemisphere. In addition, it has granted permanent observer status to 67 states, as well as to the European Union (EU).

The organisation uses a four-pronged approach to effectively implement its essential purposes, based on its main pillars: democracy, human rights, security and development.

Article 2 of the Charter of the OAS states that: "The Organization of American States, in order to put into practice the principles on which it is founded and to fulfill its regional obligations under the Charter of the United Nations, proclaims the following essential purposes:

- To strengthen the peace and security of the continent.
- To prevent possible causes of difficulties and to ensure the pacific settlement of disputes that may arise among the Member States.
- To seek the solution of political, juridical and economic problems that may arise among them.

---

[1] Evolution of OAS: International Union of American Republics... Pan American Union .... GS/OAS.

- To promote, by cooperative action, their economic, social and cultural development.
- To eradicate extreme poverty, which constitutes an obstacle to the full democratic development of the peoples of the hemisphere."

Inter American Program on Sustainable Development (PIDS) and the "Water Agenda at OAS

Water agenda at OAS is based on Mandates from their General Assembly, Ministerial declarations and agreements from the Presidential Summits of the Americas. These documents expressed the main concerns of Member States on water challenges for the hemisphere associated not only to development but also to other important determinants such as security, transparency, human rights, peace and democracy. These roads for action presented by OAS Member States indicate that the challenges of global warming and climate change, productivity and water access (health) must be faced with concrete actions leading to integral solutions which include equity, gender sensitivity, poverty reduction and security. Because these are topics which are not exclusive for developing countries, the water agenda at OAS is part of a wider hemispheric vision in which, it is recognised the differences in solution's approach from macro regions and countries in the Americas.

What comes from this understanding is certainly that water is an element for articulating peace; promote democracy and good neighbours, elements that were integrated into an Inter American Program on Sustainable Development (PIDS)[2] with specific areas of general action closely coordinated with developments in other international organisations. The OAS role in implementing PIDS should be consistent with, and complementary to, those of other relevant regional and multilateral entities, particularly with the United Nations.

Summits of the Americas (Miami,94; Santiago Chile 98; Bolivia 96; Quebec, 01; Monterrey Mexico,04; Mar del Plata 05)

Summit of the Americas on Sustainable Development (Bolivia 1996)

Inter American Council for Integral Development (CIDI)

Inter American Committee on Integral Development (CIDS)

Inter American Program on Sustainable Development (PIDS)

General Assembly resolution AG/RES.1440 (XXVI-O/96), resolution CIDI/CIDS/RES.1 (III-O/02), and Article 95 of the OAS Charter provide the necessary political background for this (PIDS) strategic plan that involves policies, programmes and projects in support of integral development.

In the particular context of OAS the organisation will:

- Serve as a hemispheric forum to promote dialogue and coordinate progress in the

[2] *First Inter-Amercican Meeting of Ministers and OEA/XLIII.1 High-LevelAuthorities on Sustainable DevelopmentCIDI/RIMDS/doc.21/06 rev. 2 December 4-5, 2006 11 May 2007 Santa Cruz de la Sierra,*

area of sustainable development.

- Support the exchange of information relating to sustainable development, and facilitate the exchange of experiences among countries, institutions, and organisations; and
- Act as a partner in cooperation among stakeholders involved in sustainable development in those areas in which the OAS General Secretariat has a comparative advantage.

The objective of the PIDS is to serve the interests of Member States by reaffirming strategic priorities of action within the overarching framework of sustainable development. The PIDS carries out its priority activities in the following specific areas:

- Sustainable agriculture and the sustainable management of forests and other natural resource.
- Water Resources, Land and Health.
- Natural Hazards Risk Management.
- Coastal Zone Management and Adaptation to Climate Change.
- Renewable Energy and Energy Efficiency Promotion.
- Capacity Building and Institutional Strengthening for Sustainable Development and Environmental Management

Based on these existing mechanisms, water diplomacy has a major and important role at OAS, contributing during all these years to reduce the effects of potential conflicts arising from a unilateral use of natural resources with important impacts on transboundary regions. When emerging water problems are associated to poverty, lack of opportunities, environmental degradation, ineffective leadership and weak political institutions, the results can lead to social decomposition and tensions which could escalate further than local. Because the OAS is a political multilateral negotiating body, the available tools for peaceful convergence and problem solution must be used.

A fundamental for water diplomacy is the possibility to have valid interactions with the determinants that are related to conflict. At the OAS, water agenda is executed in the framework of integral and sustainable development, therefore, social, economic and environmental factors converge, at the same time with education, culture, gender and security that complement the necessary ingredients for preventing water associated conflicts.

OAS water agenda is implemented at three levels: one which include the areas of cooperation (programmes and projects), where gaps on water governance exists in the hemisphere, another where there exist a dialogue space and an exchange of information, experiences and best practices takes place and third at the political level where there is convergence of results from the previous levels with the potential to reach agreements on protection, conservation and sustainable use of water resources, particularly transboundary.

At all levels, water diplomacy has a space and several particular experiences can demonstrate it. At the programme/project level, the best examples are related to changes in governments where all priority settings of governance can change, from institutions and new legislation, to financial mechanisms and participation. Priority changes can be moderated but in some cases they are major, leading to intense negotiations in order to accomplish objectives on activities already agreed by two or more parties.

Programmes and projects of large magnitude take several years to design, negotiate and implement, which bring the possibility that some change in national priorities or new transboundary agreements takes place.

Some other cases of political implications associated to water can be as old as the case of the Lauca's river dispute, 1962, between Chile and Bolivia, where Chile wanted this river to be diverted for irrigating dessert areas and Bolivia objected to same. Some similar and more recent cases exist, for example the San Juan River case associated to border demarcation between Costa Rica and Nicaragua.

An emergent issue on water resources is related to the UN General Assembly Resolution A/RES/63/124 on the Law of Transboundary Aquifers. This is an effort from UNESCO-IHP where OAS has played a significant role coordinating the ISARM-Americas programme and executing the Guarani Aquifer project that derived in the San Juan Agreement. The Law of Transboundary Aquifers is a concrete step forward towards the peaceful sharing of groundwater resources *(http://www.unesco.org/water/news/transboundaryaquifers.shtml).*

Another case where water diplomacy also has an important role is on the impacts that commercial agreements has on water governance; examples derived from United States-Central America and Dominican Republic Free Trade Agreement (US-CAFTA) is being worked at OAS.

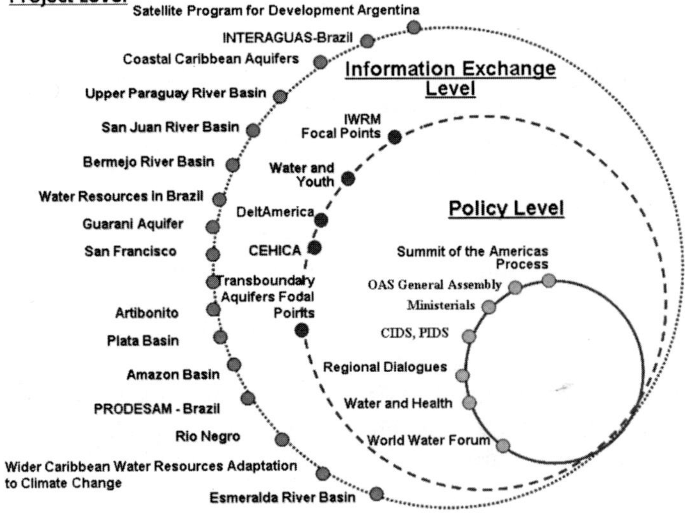

Water Management Agenda: Major Challenges and the Strategic Lines of Action where Water Diplomacy has a Fundamental Role

Water Challenges	**Strategic Lines of Action**
Global determinants: Financial, energy, health, food and climate crisis. Exponential increase of water pollution.	Promote hemispheric water security by supporting global and regional policies developed at UN and OAS in order to reduce the impacts of global crisis and their effect on water resources.
Decrease in financial investments on hydraulic projects (energy, potable water, sanitation, irrigation, tourism and recreation). Changes in water supply associated to climate variability and climate change.	Contribute in developing and implementing options and mechanisms for adaptation to climate variability and climate change impacts in water resources, particularly those that contribute building a more resilient and competitive society.
Increase in water demand due to increase in population and water associated services (hydropower, potable water, and irrigation for food production and biofuels). Water governance crisis: weak institutions, fractioned and obsolete legislation, limited financial investment and mechanisms, narrow participation of civil society (NGOs, academics, private sector) and the strong need for transparency and accountability.	To increase the exchange of experiences, good practices on Water Governance for an effective implementation of IWRM among OAS Member States. To facilitate the interaction between government and the main water actors
Limited vision of regional opportunities: few agreements on protection, conservation and sustainable use of transboundary waters in the hemisphere.	To promote "water as a means to promote peace and democracy" in the agenda of bi-national and regional institutions in the hemisphere. To support OAS Member States in the negotiation process taking place at the UN regarding transboundary waters

Emerging Challenges for Water Diplomacy in the Americas

In a scenario of 20 to 30 years, it can be guessed that the actual water policies related to costs and investments in infrastructure are not going to change significantly, as well the cultural rules that many times determine water policies will continue even though some social perturbations take place, and also countries with a solid economic growth will continue making investments in infrastructure and technology to meet their own water challenges. The resulting scenario is that water supply will not meet the demand due to lack of efficient management of resources, i.e., water problems will make the key countries producing food and energy putting in risk the global food markets and limiting economic growth. At the same time, the water resources in the transboundary regions (superficial and aquifers) will grow in importance and become political influential hot spots. Another consequence is associated to the potential increase in water disease, again, limiting productivity and producing economic impacts.

The traditional dialogue about security in the Americas is migrating from the traditional themes of war and peace toward the relationship between man and environment, therefore the ability for countries of managing shared resources in a politically sustainable matter, i.e. with minimum tensions, is evolving, however there are still new challenges that might need an intense and robust water diplomacy in which the OAS could play an important role.

✧

MONSOONS
THE ECONOMY WELCOMES THE FINANCE MINISTER

HYDRO ETHICS
HYDRO PHILOSOPHY
HYDRO CALLOUSNESS
HYDRO INTELLIGENCE
HYDRO COMMON SENSE
HYDRO RIGHTS
HYDRO POLITICS
HYDRO SOCIOLOGY
HYDRO COMPETITION
HYDRO SOLIDARITY
HYDRO DIPLOMACY
HYDRO PERSUASION
HYDRO LOGIC

SHARING WATER ACROSS BORDERS

Basin Organisations and Transboundary Rivers

Ian W Makin

Introduction

Water scarcity and pollution, population growth, urbanisation, environmental degradation, floods, and climate change are all issues that are emerging as concerns that result in increased water-related tensions. Such tensions are beginning to drive changes to how countries address water management. Integrated water resources management (IWRM) is widely accepted as the most-effective management model to help water resource managers and users resolve, often, conflicting objectives within a river basin.

The Asian Water Development Outlook (Asian Development Bank, 2013) published by the Asian Development Bank (ADB) and the Asia Pacific Water Forum (APWF) provides a quantitative estimate of water security in the Asia and Pacific region. By effectively measuring the tensions that result from allocations to different water uses, the AWDO water security tools provide a five dimensional framework to assess the outcome of IWRM.

In Asia and the Pacific region, the evolution of the institutions responsible for the development and management of a majority of river basins has generally led to each having a distinct mandate. The division of responsibilities between agencies has made effective integration of planning and activities inadequate to meet the challenges that are emerging in many basins, including population growth, rural to urban migration, increasing wastewater discharge, climate change and related increases in extreme events. The institutional difficulties are made more challenging when the river basin spans administrative boundaries, whether these are a local or an international boundary.

The concept of hydro-diplomacy expands beyond the water managers comfort zone of the water management sciences to involve, in the case of international rivers, consideration of sovereignty, political dimensions, and concerns about national security as well as economic outcomes of water investments and decisions. The paper presents some thoughts on necessary conditions for appropriate river governance and effective hydro-diplomacy in both sub-national and international trans-boundary rivers.

Dimensions of Trans-boundary Rivers

It is almost inevitable when the subject of trans-boundary river is considered, the challenges of the international rivers, such as the Indus, Ganges, Mekong, Nile, Okavango, Syr Darya, Amu Darya, Rhine and Danube are often uppermost in most people's minds (International Water Association, 2013). However, while these and similar rivers have challenged, and in many cases continue to challenge, the capacity and creativity of the agencies responsible for their management, there are many thousands of smaller rivers, crossing sub-national boundaries which also pose complex management challenges. For this paper, let us consider the issues that all boundaries pose for river and water resource managers, and how hydro-diplomacy can help resolve potential disputes.

A useful definition of a trans-boundary river is—sources of freshwater that are shared among multiple user groups, with diverse values and different needs associated with water use (Universities Partnership for Transboundary Waters, 2013). This definition allows us to consider the way water crosses boundaries—whether these are between economic actors and sectors, across legal jurisdictions, or political interests. It also means that, effectively, all freshwaters are trans-boundary in some way and calls for managers that fully appreciate that water is important to society at local, national, regional, and international scales. It also means that basin managers must understand the complexities of interests in the basin and how individual decisions impact on other users and interested parties. This highlights the critical need for integrated planning, decision-making and management of water resources—in short why IWRM is required for effective management and why river managers must think outside the 'water-box'.

The background information for the 2012 Chaing Rai conference on Hydro-diplomacy summarised hydro-diplomacy as "going beyond the science of water management to involve sovereignty, political, security as well as economic considerations". There is no contradiction between the objectives, and ideally, the approaches of IWRM and hydro-diplomacy. For efficient and productive use of water the management organisations, responsible for water allocation and control with the basin, must be responsive to the needs of the population, economies and eco-systems within the basin.

The UN Convention of Non-Navigational Use of International Watercourses (1997), although not yet ratified, sets out the guiding principles for trans-boundary governance as: (i) equitable and reasonable use and (ii) a commitment not to cause significant harm. These principles are equally valid for boundaries between users and between administrations within a nation. Unfortunately, where water has been delegated to local administrations, the urgent need to accelerate economic growth and poverty reduction can lead to decisions that fail these principles, particularly when decisions are made based on narrow technical assessments of water availability without adequate analysis of existing use or downstream impacts.

The use of hydro-diplomacy to describe trans-boundary management does have the advantage of raising the discussion from a purely technical water resources issue to become more inclusive, with political and legal participation. A participant at a trans-boundary meeting recalled his first experience at a meeting of parties that shared a substantial river, "...we arrived well briefed with five engineers, but the delegation from the downstream team arrived with one engineer and five lawyers. We learnt from that and now include a solid legal team in all meetings...".

Effective river basin decisions require managers to have a firm understanding of the various uses and interests in the water resources of the river and not only within their own jurisdiction. For example, in a recent dispute between two sub-national states, the upstream state mobilised experienced irrigation agronomists to make "informal" surveys of the crop stage and irrigated area in the downstream state. The survey, backed up by use of analysis of very recent remote sensing data, provided the basis for the political, technical and legal negotiators to challenge the claimed downstream water requirements. This illustrates how local administrative boundaries can be as contentious as international boundaries. With increasing numbers of river basins facing increasingly frequent occurrences of water stress due to growing populations with changing diets, growing economies, and the impacts of climate change, managers will increasingly need to apply the tools of hydro-diplomacy to resolve disputes.

International and sub-national administrative boundaries rarely align fully with the natural catchment boundaries of rivers; hence the need for trans-boundary management. Unfortunately, the administrative boundaries of sector agencies often do not align well with either the natural catchment or the spatial responsibilities of other agencies. This overlays a further level of complexity in basin decision-making and is the driving logic for some form of basin organisation that can "cut-through" the bureaucracy in existing sector agencies to seek "more optimal" outcomes. However, we must recognise such river basin organisations (RBOs) currently have a mixed level of success, depending to a large extent of the distribution of power among the agencies and administrations. Also, overlaying RBO over local administration requires care to avoid weakening the principles of management at the "lowest appropriate level".

Where there are large asymmetries of power within the basin—whether between countries or provinces as a result of upstream control of headwaters relative to downstream dependency, or between economic uses, hydropower entities can exert very strong asymmetric economic power to determine how water is allocated. Or as Reisner (1986) summarised the situation—water can defy gravity and flow uphill to money and power.

Making Trans-boundary River Basin Governance Work

Whether considering a major international river, a river shared between sub-national states, or determining water allocation between competing users, the reality is that institutions are making critical decisions about land and water issues without a full appreciation of the overall basin situation.

As demands increase, water resources become increasingly stressed, leading to increased competition among users and riparian administrations. On occasion the popular media raise the potential for future water conflicts to become water wars. Current experience has demonstrated that, even where expanding population and water demands have out-grown available water resources to the extent of raising the potential for conflict, to date, virtual water trade particularly in food has avoided such an outcome. This trade has also disguised the asymmetry of power among the stakeholders involved as managers and political leaders seek to avoid potential conflicts (Zeitoun et al, 2008).

As we look to the future of water governance, some key principles can be proposed that should guide trans-boundary management, whether between agencies, sub-national administrative regions or international rivers. These principles include recognition that water is a truly "shared" natural resource where equitable outcomes can be achieved where:

- There is an adequate knowledge of:
    - o how much water is in the basin,
    - o how it is being used, and
    - o who has existing rights to use it

- Stakeholders are committed to seeking to share-benefits of water use.
- Clearly agreed "rules of the game" among stakeholders.
- Decisions are built on the principles of Equity and Mutual Respect.

Although there are many existing competent agencies responsible for the management of water resources and water services in river basins, as water resources become an ever more binding constraint to development, the need for river basin organisations to take a lead in the planning and allocation of water use becomes more urgent.

Water is critical for life and, in some way or other; it plays a role in almost all economic activities. Water also plays a critical role in determining the quality of the environment in which we live. As such, people and agencies tend to be very possessive about their water responsibilities, resisting change and aggressively defending their use and stewardship of this critical resource.

It is not surprising then that the creation of over-arching RBOs is not easy and new organisations are likely to face considerable resistance from existing sector agencies. New skills outside the water specialists' standard 'toolkit', including the capacity for hydro-diplomacy, are urgently needed if the water challenges of the coming decades are to be resolved efficiently and equitably whether for negotiations between sector agencies, across provincial boundaries, or in international river dialogues.

Future of Water Security

Water security is an essential foundation for sustainable economic development and requires water sector leaders to develop the necessary skills, knowledge and commitment to:

Achieve consensus	-	about what are the objectives for water resources management in the basin.
Build capacities	-	for effective IWRM and hydro-diplomacy among riparian agencies and stakeholders.
Coordinate actions	-	across sector and administrative jurisdictions.
Define development	-	as the successful outcome of coordinated efforts that result in shared costs and benefits for stakeholders of shared water resources.

Water is increasingly recognised as a critical and potentially binding constraint in many countries and basins. Given the important role of water in economic activity, it is not surprising that private sector entities are beginning to focus on water in order to protect an increasingly critical input to their production processes. While some stakeholders consider engagement of commercial firms in water resources as a potentially dangerous innovation; the challenge of finding efficient and effective mechanisms to improve the stewardship of water and river basin eco-systems is such that the considerable management, research and financial resources of the private sector may provide valuable "new tools" in the search for sustainable trans-boundary water resources management at local, national and international scales.

References

Asian Development Bank (2013). *Asian Water Development Outlook 2013. 2nd Print. April. Available at: http://www.adb.org/publications/asian-water-development-outlook-2013 (accessed 21 October 2013)*

International Water Association (n.d.) Water WIKI: *Transboundary Rivers. Available at: http://www.iwawaterwiki.org/xwiki/bin/view/Articles/Trans-boundaryWaterManagement (accessed 21 October 2013)*

Reisner, M. (1986). Cadillac Desert: *The American West and its Disappearing Water.* New York, USA: Penguin Books,

Universities Partnership for Transboundary Waters (n.d.). *http://waterpartners.geo.orst.edu/faq.html (accessed 21 October 2013)*

Zeitoun, Mark and J.A. Allan (2008). *"Applying hegemony and power theory to transboundary water analysis", Water Policy 10(2): 3-12. Available at: http://www.uea.ac.uk/polopoly_fs/1.147022!ZeitounAllan_Power_Hegemony_Theory_HH_Special_Issue.pdf (accessed 21 October 2013)*

?
No.
No water.
Only methane

HYDRO ETHICS
HYDRO PHILOSOPHY
HYDRO CALLOUSNESS
HYDRO INTELLIGENCE
HYDRO COMMON SENSE
HYDRO RIGHTS
HYDRO POLITICS
HYDRO SOCIOLOGY
HYDRO COMPETITION
HYDRO SOLIDARITY
HYDRO DIPLOMACY
HYDRO PERSUASION
HYDRO LOGIC

SHARING WATER
ACROSS BORDERS

A Review of the Institutional Framework for Management of Water Resources in the Ganges-Brahmaputra-Meghna System

Ainun Nishat

I WAS involved in the negotiation process, for arriving at agreed solutions for management of water resources of rivers, common between India and Bangladesh, over a long period of time. To be more specific, I was a Member of the Indo-Bangladesh Joint River Commission (JRC) for 18 years, till end of 1999. JRC is the institution mandated for conducting the discussions between the two countries. I am not aware of any significant change in the approach followed for discussions as well as in the role of the key actors, since I moved out of the process. In my view, the role the JRC play, presently, is different from the role that was envisaged from this institution when it was setup in 1972. It was supposed to be a platform for working out options that will facilitate cooperation in management of the common rivers. But by 1974, within 3 years of its life, it was pushed in the direction of confrontation and since then, it has become a platform for hard negotiation, based mainly on technical approach.

Recently, we have noticed major changes in the political commitment as revealed in the Framework Agreement on Cooperation and Development between Bangladesh and India, finalised and signed in September 2011. Will the present institutional arrangement and its approach bring success in satisfactory development and management of water resources of common rivers of the region, taking into account the changes in the political level? The main objective of this brief note is to propose appropriate changes in the institutional framework, currently in place.

If a river traverses over two or more sovereign countries, or, two or more states of a federal type government, then involvement of all the co-riparian countries/states are to be ensured in planning, development and management of the water resources of the common river, in order to ensure a basin wide approach. Such an approach is recommended in all text-books and multi-lateral environmental agreements. For such rivers cooperation among two or more than two countries, as the case may be, will be required; in case of states of a federal type country, almost similar approach will be necessary, though political constraints may be less challenging. In all cases political decisions must guide the consultation process and, if necessary, be able to over-ride technical as well so-called legal arguments. As I have not noticed any significant change in institutional framework, I remain dismayed about the progress in the discussionprocess, despite a major break-through in the political arena.

Bangladesh is the lower riparian of three major rivers of the world namely the Ganges, the Brahmaputra and the Meghna. These three rivers along with their distributaries and tributaries form the Ganges-Brahmaputra-Meghna (GBM) system. The GBM system in Bangladesh carries about 92 per cent of the total flow from across the border. For the country, it is imperative to achieve cooperation of upper riparian countries for optimum utilisation of her water resources.

Presently, Bangladesh has to be content in developing the water resources within its territory and has to limit the level of development within the resources available in the country. The temporal distribution remains a major challenge in water management. In other words we have constructed embankments and polders for flood management but could not go for reservoirs and watershed management for lowering the peak flow. The earthen dykes that are the main instruments for flood management are fragile and breaches during high flood resulting them to be redundant. River bank erosion remains a serious problem as the fury of the river remains unabated as the flow cannot be controlled in the monsoon months. For irrigation, the country mainly concentrates on harvesting of groundwater though the annual volume of surface water that flows through the country is huge. Volume of groundwater that may be pumped out is also reaching the level of saturation. Therefore, Bangladesh must make every effort to harvest surface water that will require cooperation of upper riparian countries.

All the text-books and recommendations of various organs of the United Nations such as UNWater, UNDP, FAO and many resolutions of the UN General Assembly call for a basin approach in trans-boundary water management. Civil society organisations such as Global Water Partnership, World Water Council also plead for basin-wise approach in water management. Agenda 21 makes strong water recommendation in this direction.

While there is a consensus in the global level on the need to push for a basin approach and noting that such an approach has been formally accepted at the highest political level between India and Bangladesh, I feel encouraged and I feel a wind of change in the right direction.

I am referring to the "Framework Agreement on Cooperation for Development" between Bangladesh and India, signed by the two Prime Ministers in September 2011. Article 2 of this Agreement states that "to enhance cooperation in sharing of the waters of common rivers, both parties (India and Bangladesh) will explore the possibilities of common basin management of common rivers for mutual benefits." This decision, to me, is a landmark decision. I believe that the spirit of cooperation that existed between India and the newly immersed country Bangladesh in early 70's, has been rekindled.

This made me think, will this decision be implemented with due urgency and diligently. Unfortunately I think that unless there is a major shift in the institutional framework in discussions, no significant deviation will happen in the existing trend and results. As of today, it appears that the JRC will remain in charge of taking forward the directives contained in the Article 2 of the 2011 Framework for Cooperation. I strongly argue for a change in the institutional framework. We need to bring in the political dimension of the decision-taking process in the institutional framework and put it on the top of the technical and legal deliberations. Of course the political process will take into account the technical and legal arguments. But the flexibility and quid-pro-quo in the results has to be directed by the political masters.

Let us look into the process of setting up of the JRC in 1972 by a decision of the Prime Ministers of the two countries; and it started functioning immediately. The Statutes of the JRC were finalised 9 months later, in November 1972 and a spirit of cooperation and collaboration prevailed in the initial days. The preamble of this document contains the vision for setting up this institution. It stated that the JRC was set up being "desirous in working together in harnessing the rivers common to both countries for the benefit of people of the two countries". The functions of the JRC were stipulated through five mandates. First mandate stipulated that the JRC would "maintain liaison between participating countries in order to ensure that the most effective joint efforts in maximising the benefits from the common river systems to both countries." The other four mandates related to various aspects of flood control works. One would recall in the 60's and 70's flood was recognised as the key concern in water resources management. In those days, aus (also known as kharif I) and aman (also known as kharif II) were the two paddy growing seasons of the country, aman being the main crop, Aus usually grown between April/May to July/August and Aman is grown between July/August to November/December. Crops grown in both the periods, cover the monsoon season, could be damaged by flood; they are essentially rain-fed with occasional demand of supplementary irrigation. The paddy-growing season in the winter/dry months is known as Boro/Robi. Currently, Boro is the main crop of Bangladesh but at the time when JRC was set up, coverage of land by Boro paddy was very small. Therefore, obviously flood management received top attention. Attention given to other issues with respect to water resources management like irrigation, fisheries development, navigation, industrial water supply, rural and urban water supply and sanitation, ecosystem management etc., was almost nil.

The composition of the JRC is very interesting; each country is to have a Chairperson/Co-chairman and three Members, two of them will be professional engineers. (I was one of them between 1981-1999.) Initially the Chairperson/Co-chairpersons were the Secretary, Ministry of Water Resources of the two countries;

since 1977 the Ministers for Water Resources of the two countries are functioning as the chair and co-chair alternatively. In the initial days of JRC, the approach of collaboration prevailed and efforts were made to develop joint projects. Being part of the system and having observed it functioning from within the institution, I can safely say that all deliberations were based on technical considerations. However, all major agreements that have been reached, so far, had happened, only when directives from political masters were available. This is the limitation of the current institution and there is no mechanism for regular consultation between the political and technical platforms. I have mentioned earlier that by 1974, JRC was converted into a platform for negotiations when sharing of waters of the Ganges became a hot agenda and deliberations on augmentation of its flow were initiated. As a result, the institution set up in March 1972 to carry out technical consultation for development of water resources of common rivers lost its sight on the mandate for which it was set up. Political consultations are held on ad-hoc basis. Progress in water talks is rather unsatisfactory in the eyes of common citizens as they notice some forward movement only when instructions are delivered from political level.

Therefore, for implementation of the landmark decision of the Prime Ministers of the two countries, it is important that we look into the institutional mechanism. In my view, two mechanisms or institutions will be necessary; one for technical aspects, other for political aspects. The technical/professional body must be able to recommend alternatives and options to the political body, for maximising benefit from the common water resources, on a basin-wide and basis-wise approach, independent of the political position of co-riparian countries. This would require participation of India, Bangladesh and Nepal to take forward the discussions on the Ganges; and, participation of Bhutan, India, Bangladesh and China for the Brahmaputra River. For all other rivers, talks may take place between Bangladesh and India, as only these two countries are the co-basin countries, on river by river basis, for each of the 50 common rivers. The technical body should move away from the current approach of working out share of flow available at the border. Development of options and plans for management of the common rivers on a "basin wise" and "basin wide" approach should be the goal of the technical/ professional unit. It will be prudent to set up two separate technical units for the Ganges and the Brahmaputra, respectively. Consultations for other common rivers may be held on another platform.

The professional bodies may be called River Basin Authority/ Commission and must be able to function independently to reach their goal on the basis of their mandate. The second mechanism to be developed will provide political guidance to the technical/professional bodies and the final decision should rest on political masters. River Basin Authority/Commission as may be set up will have separate technical and political platforms. Obviously the political body will contain representatives of all co-riparian countries. The technical body must be managed as a professional organisation.

We may draw lessons from the US-Mexico Water and Boundary Commission,

Rhine River Commission, Mekong River Commission, Snowy Mountain River Commission, etc., for setting its modus operandi. Independent professionals may be engaged for technical analysis and formulation of options. Involvement of UN agencies and countries from outside the region should be welcome. At the political level, the concerned political decision-makers may be encouraged to study how similar issues have been resolved in other river basins of the world.

We need to make a breakthrough in the present level of impasse in the water talks. Transparency in the discussion making process must be ensured in order to gain confidence of the citizens; and, availability of data and outcome of technical analyses must be ensured. Actually the wind of change at the political level became visible in the Joint Declarations issued after the visit to India by the Prime Minister of Bangladesh in January 2010; this trend was maintained in the Joint Statement issued September 2011, after the visit of Prime Minister of India to Bangladesh. The two joint statements mentioned collaborations in the fields of navigation, riverbank erosion control and dredging, ecosystem management, climate change, flood forecasting and flood management, etc.

One issue that must receive urgent attention is the goal stipulated in Article-6 of the 2011 Framework for Cooperation that aims to "preserve a common ecosystem." This is a significant decision that water of common rivers should be developed not only for the benefit of the two countries but also for the protection of the ecosystem. I would also like to put emphasis on navigation through the river network both for domestic as well as trans-country traffic. Till 1965 when navigation between the then East Pakistan and India was suspended, all the three major river systems, the Ganges and the Brahmaputra and the Meghna carried riverine vessels from one part of India to another part through Bangladesh. The huge potential of hydropower may be harnessed by paying attention to geologic (earthquake), social (including resettlement) and environmental consideration. Ever increasing shortfall in energy production in the region can easily be met if the huge potential of hydropower available in the upper reaches of the rivers is harnessed. Construction dams and water storage reservoirs will produce commercial energy and ensure sufficient draft for navigation and protect eco-system of the mangroves.

To conclude, let me make the following points:

- The effectiveness of the present modus operandi in the JRC may be evaluated and new institutional frameworks for management for common rivers on basin-wise and basin-wide approach need to be established with separation of technical functions from political process, with the later having control over final decisions.

- Seasonal and temporal variation in availability of water will be a critical factor in future and annual average flow does not reflect the true ground condition. The looming threat of climate change and climate variability must be taken seriously as this will disrupt and disturb the current hydrological cycle and availability of water in a predictable manner.

- Benefits from hydropower may be realised, but in the process environmental and social considerations must be rigorously upheld. Provision of e-flow for managing ecosystem must be made in the development process and opportunities of navigation must be harnessed.

- Transparency in all decisions made will lead to building confidence among common people.

The provisions with respects to management of common rivers as contained in the 2011 Framework for Cooperation are bold decisions. The political masters have given directives that are in line with the global approaches, and indicate major shift at the policy level. Without setting effective institutional mechanisms, right from the beginning, we may not benefit from the fruits of the landmark decisions.

✧

We believe in the FREE market.
BOSS
FREE to steal local water.
BOSS
FREE to exploit water resources across borders.
BOSS
Rustam

HYDRO ETHICS
HYDRO PHILOSOPHY
HYDRO CALLOUSNESS
HYDRO INTELLIGENCE
HYDRO COMMON SENSE
HYDRO RIGHTS
HYDRO POLITICS
HYDRO SOCIOLOGY
HYDRO COMPETITION
HYDRO SOLIDARITY
HYDRO DIPLOMACY
HYDRO PERSUASION
HYDRO LOGIC

SHARING WATER ACROSS BORDERS

Hydro-Diplomacy: The Political, Normative and Institutional Dimensions

Alejandro Iza

HYDRO-DIPLOMACY is a tool for implementing effective water governance.

One of the most important aspects of hydro-diplomacy is international cooperation applied to water resources extending beyond the borders of one country. Cooperation is also one of the fundamental principles of international law and it can be seen as a continuous process, a relation between two or more States which ideally get together to talk, consult each other and agree on how to address common problems and opportunities.

International cooperation requires and is facilitated by the existence of three different dimensions: political, normative and institutional. These three dimensions operate at various levels: local, national, regional and international. In order to be more specific and to avoid ambiguity, I will try to define these dimensions and then contextualise them in a trans-boundary basin.

Policy is the blueprint for drafting and amending the law since it is adjustable over time and can be used to experiment solutions on the ground before crystallising them into fixed provisions. However, policy offers a discrete amount of certainty by establishing and defining a clear set of goals that have to be pursued in a certain period of time.

Policy formulation mobilises citizen and public involvement and is guided—or should be guided—by internationally accepted principles such as equity and sustainability. Its implementation requires more and more an adequate level of decentralisation. This is particularly important in managing natural resources as the "one size fits all approach" does not always work. Natural resources, in fact, need to be managed respecting the surrounding context (not only in environmental terms, but also in population and economic terms). Therefore, and although the decision and actions taken need to be framed in a broader vision that respect the unity of the basin, they must be "tailored" to the specific conditions of the environment. In other words, a holistic view has to be reconciled with local realities to work effectively. In the context of shared basins, one of the most important political instruments is the basin plan which defines the strategies to adopt and medium/long term objectives for a specific period of time. Such a plan is the result of political negotiations among the basin countries; it needs to be developed along the lines of legal provisions contained in the basin agreement and has to be implemented by the basin authority.

Law is by definition long lasting and brings certainty, establishing a framework under which water institutions and agencies can operate. The law determines a system of water rights and establishes rules for water appropriation. It promotes conservation of water resources through systems of command and control and market-based incentives.

Water law should be synchronised with other natural resources laws. This horizontal coherence (horizontal because it refers to legislations of multiple sectors operating at the same governance level, for example national or regional or international) should be accompanied by vertical coherence which refers to water instruments operating at different governance level. For instance, a basin agreement needs to be developed according to international principles and has to be implemented at national level through ad hoc actions that might also have legal nature.

The law of the basins is primarily the basin agreements, which constitute the framework for regulating state actions and for managing it. They are complemented by the creation of a basin institution and the development of a set of political and technical instruments (basin development plan, strategic actions etc.) adjustable to the multiple challenges, needs and conditions of the basin.

Institutions represent the operative arm of the dimensions mentioned before, since they are the fundamental means to deliver policy and law. Again, there is a variety of institutions operating at different administrative levels. The challenge is to achieve a certain degree of institutional coordination in order to avoid fragmented actions and the pursuing of contrasting objectives.

Water institutions have multiple functions, for example planning and coordinating, fostering public participation, operating and maintaining water works, or administering water rights and permits. In trans-boundary basins, the creation of a common authority should promote the integrated planning and management of trans-boundary waters and related resources through an effective implementation of the basin development plan and other relevant actions.

It is evident that policy, law and institutions are not separate silos but interconnected dimensions that are fundamental to each other and might fit together in different ways. But capacity or capacities are needed to ensure this inter-connection to be effective and deliver sustainability and justice.

This is the reason why we propose that policy, Law and Institutions are the pillars of water governance capacity or the competence of a society to implement effective water management by means of transparent, coherent, and cost efficient policy, law and institutions. Policy and law provide the skeleton that is fleshed out by institutions and management practices.

Although we know the medicine, it is not always easy to prescribe it. On more than 260 shared basins, only 55 count with a cooperative agreement while 158 do not have any kind of cooperative scheme at all. The lack of a framework compromises the effective management of these shared resources and ultimately has a crucial impact on their sustainable use.

Ideally basin agreements would be inspired by and should contain provisions reflecting the content of fundamental principles such as:

- Cooperation and good neighbourliness.
- Equitable and reasonable utilisation.
- Duty not to cause (sensible) harm.
- Integrated management.
- Ecosystems protection.
- Sustainability.
- Participation.
- Information exchange, consultation and negotiation.

Explaining each one of these principles in detail would require multiple and extensive lectures and we do not actually have all that time. However, we should highlight the fact that these principles are already included in a variety of international, regional and national legal instruments, and inform the develop of new ones.

Among these instruments, there is the 1997 UN Convention on the Law of the Non-Navigational Uses of International Watercourses which can be seen as a framework and guiding instrument for the development of new basin agreements. This Convention is not yet into force, but many of the principles contained therein are recognised as part of customary international law.

Another reference document is the 1992 UNECE Convention on the Protection and Use of Trans-boundary Watercourse and International Lakes, which is still a regional agreement but will be soon open to non-UNECE members, and could become a global reference instrument. The UNECE Convention contains stricter and more specific provisions on monitoring, research and development, consultations, warning and alarm systems, mutual assistance, and exchange of information, as well as access to information by the public. It has been in force for a decade and it has proved to be beneficial for strengthening national measures for the protection and ecologically sound management of trans-boundary surface waters and groundwaters, improving trans-boundary cooperation.

The two Conventions present differences and similarities but are not competing with each other, instead they could be seen as mutually reinforcing instruments.

Beyond these two conventions there are other regional or basin cooperative frameworks that could serve as an example (the MRC, the NBI, the Titicaca, the Danube, the Volta are just few examples). The point here is not only to see if these agreements tell successful stories, but also to highlight the good manifested by the States that started collaborating; their understanding of the unified character of a basin and the need to face common challenges and opportunities together; the process of negotiating, trading off, and sharing benefits. All this is a good story at the end of the day.

As I´ve already mentioned cooperation is an ongoing process, a flow, a continuum. This means that it is constituted by numerous and different activities which carry a lower or higher degree of integration between States' actions, which are part of the water basin. In the first stage, States can assure communications and notifications, and they can also guarantee mutual access to information and the development of regional consultations. A higher level of cooperation carries the implementation of national projects with cooperative benefits and the adaptation of national plans to reduce costs and perceive regional benefits. The maximum level of cooperation leads to joint project design, and to joint institutions and property. This tells us that countries get motivated in reinforcing cooperation when they see and understand hydro-diplomacy, that is, sharing brings more benefits than acting unilaterally.

Once they enter into agreements or, in general, why do State abide by these rules and international principles?

There are different reasons which belong to a diplomatic or a legal sphere. In diplomatic terms, States respect the rules as they want to avoid being exposed to criticism and shame in the international community. In addition, they want to avoid "sanctions" from the international community (sanctions of economical or political nature like lower level of trades or even embargos and similar actions). So, if a contrast arises, at first States resort to alternative methods of conciliation such as negotiation, good offices of a third party, mediation and arbitration. However, there might be stronger let's call them "incentives" to cooperate and respect the rules. Indeed, States are (or should be) interested in doing what is lawful and right and they are particularly keen on avoiding being sued by other States or suffering the potential sanctions established by a court (in particular the International Court of Justice, which is the highest juridical authority at the international level) or other tribunals (which might be created ad hoc).

It can be considered good practice to include provisions on settling disputes within a bi-national/regional/international agreement in order to establish clear rules on how to face challenging situations and contrasts. As to say, in every basin (when regulated) it is essential and beneficial, in terms of legal certainty and security, to have a "sophisticated" dispute settlement mechanism to resolve conflicts of interpretation and application of the rules. In some cases, like in the Pulp Mills case—Argentina and Uruguay, and aside from the conflict itself, the States have reached such a level of maturity in their bilateral relations that they have accepted the jurisdiction, therefore the future decision, of an international tribunal.

And finally, we can stress over and over again that in essence hydro-diplomacy in action, that is cooperation, is beneficial for all the stakeholders involved— international, national and local, as it implies sharing burdens and costs but, above, all benefits.

✧

IDEAL

REALITY

HYDRO ETHICS
HYDRO PHILOSOPHY
HYDRO CALLOUSNESS
HYDRO INTELLIGENCE
HYDRO COMMON SENSE
HYDRO RIGHTS
HYDRO POLITICS
HYDRO SOCIOLOGY
HYDRO COMPETITION
HYDRO SOLIDARITY
HYDRO DIPLOMACY
HYDRO PERSUASION
HYDRO LOGIC

SHARING WATER
ACROSS BORDERS

Hydro-diplomacy for Better Transboundary Water Management

Khaled M. Abu Zeid

MANY OF the world's freshwater basins are shared by two or more countries. There are about 261 trans-boundary river and lake basins shared by over 145 countries, where a third of which are shared by more than two countries. There are also about 318 trans-boundary groundwater aquifers worldwide.

A small number of these basins are governed by basin agreements and treaties, but the majority is not. And even the ones that have legal frameworks in place sometimes face serious challenges. Conflicts over trans-boundary waters can be attributed to disagreements on shares of consumptive uses and abstractions for irrigated agriculture, municipal and industrial withdrawals which is usually the case in water scarce regions. Or conflicts may be related to non-consumptive uses such as pollution, storage for hydropower, or impacts on navigational uses. And sometimes conflicts may be driven by the combined effect and the interrelation between both non-consumptive and consumptive uses in riparian countries. The most serious conflicts are the ones that affect consumptive uses or water shares, since they usually affect basic human needs such as domestic water supply and subsistent agriculture. This does not discount conflicts related to non-consumptive uses, but it's just that they are easier to manage.

At the international level, the world still lacks a legal framework that is universally acceptable and technically sound to manage trans-boundary waters in an equitable manner. The 1966 Helsinki Rules, which has a lot of sound principles, have been widely used and considered until the recent UN Convention on the Law of Non-navigational Uses of International Watercourses, was adopted by the UN General Assembly in May 1997. However, 15 years later, now in 2012, 27 countries only have ratified or joined the convention so far, while the number required for the convention to come in force is 35 out of the 194 UN countries.

The current contracting States (in order of ratification) of the 1997 Convention are: "12" in Europe: Finland, Hungary, Norway, Sweden, Netherlands, Portugal, Germany, Spain, Greece, France,

Denmark, and Luxembourg, "9" in Africa: South Africa, Namibia, Libya, Tunisia, Guinea-Bissau, Nigeria, Burkina Faso, Morocco and Benin, and only "6" in Asia: Iraq, Jordan, Lebanon, Syria, Qatar and Uzbekistan (5 of which are from the Arab Region).

If one examines the water conditions of the current contracting states to the convention, one can see that some of them do not have any trans-boundary rivers; in fact some do not have any rivers at all. Some states faces serious trans-boundary water issues and feel desperate for an international legal framework that can presumably grant them some water rights. Some States are water abundant and do not face trans-boundary consumptive use water issues and may not be affected one way or another by ratifying the convention. The convention is only binding to those States that have ratified it, and so far none of the watercourses shared by the contracting States has all its riparian States party to the convention. This raises the question of whether this low number of "relevant" contracting States will render the convention unable to resolve the real conflicts that exist in the 'hot trans-boundary" rivers of the world.

On the other hand, some States argue that the convention should have been addressed at the river basin level and not at the watercourse level. Some argue that the Convention did not recognise sovereignty rights, and favoured prior appropriation. Others argue that prior appropriation of rainfed green cover waters within river basins and the availability of other water resources within the States are not sufficiently or appropriately recognised among the equitable and reasonable utilisation factors. Do these different opinions or different interpretations question the effectiveness of the implementation of this international convention if it comes into force?

Nothing will be more effective for reaching consensus on trans-boundary water management agreements other than for the riparian States to sit together and exercise hydro-diplomacy. Hydro-diplomacy is about realising win-win solutions. It's about putting political differences behind and putting mutual benefits ahead. It's about equitable sharing not equal shares. It's about joint development projects, jointly financed, jointly managed, jointly monitored, and jointly shared in profits. Hydro-diplomacy is about sharing benefits beyond the river. It's about sharing benefits as opposed to sharing water.

So, in any trans-boundary river basin, while rainfed agriculture using rainfall "green water" may be suitable for upstream States, irrigated agriculture using surface and groundwater "blue water" may be suitable for downstream States. While livestock grazing on rainfed range lands may have a comparative advantage in upstream countries, virtual water imports of livestock from upstream countries may be appropriate for downstream countries. While "blue water" in surface rivers may be used for generating hydropower in upstream States, it could run through for irrigation in downstream countries. Also, part of the generated hydropower upstream may be traded with downstream countries. Generated hydropower upstream could also be used for groundwater abstraction for supplemental irrigation in "green water" rainfed agriculture areas upstream, without affecting existing uses from "blue water" in rivers downstream.

Technically feasible, economically viable, environmentally sound, and socially acceptable solutions are possible. They need the political will to balance national interests in shared waters while ensuring mutual benefits, and that is part of hydro-diplomacy. Lack of trust can be a major impediment to achieving the kind of consensus that's required for maximising shared benefits, and trust building is definitely part of hydro-diplomacy.

Regional and developmental organisations have a role to play in advancing hydro-diplomacy. They have to work on bringing riparian States closer rather than widening the gap between them. They should maintain neutral positions that are based on scientific facts, proper hydrological assessments, and actual information on consumptive and non-consumptive uses. They can conduct unbiased baseline assessments of potential water resources within river basins including rainfall, surface water, and groundwater, and of sectoral uses by each riparian State from every water source in the basin. Regional organisations should encourage and enhance the flow and transparency of this basic information among States as it represents the first step in the right direction of hydro-diplomacy.

✧

LIVE TO SHARE!
SHARE TO LIVE!
GLOBAL WATER POLICE
Rustam

HYDRO ETHICS
HYDRO PHILOSOPHY
HYDRO CALLOUSNESS
HYDRO INTELLIGENCE
HYDRO COMMON SENSE
HYDRO RIGHTS
HYDRO POLITICS
HYDRO SOCIOLOGY
HYDRO COMPETITION
HYDRO SOLIDARITY
HYDRO DIPLOMACY
HYDRO PERSUASION
HYDRO LOGIC

SHARING WATER ACROSS BORDERS

Working towards Potential Conflict to Cooperation Potential

Léna Salamé

Complex Background

Very little freshwater is available for use, and easily accessible to humankind (approximately 0.07% of the total amount of water available on Earth is easily accessible for direct human use). Forty years ago, 12000 m3 of freshwater was available in average per year and per person. Today only 5000 m3 is available in average per year and per person. However, the total amount of water on the globe has been the same since the times of the dinosaurs.

The difference in water availability in time and space is mainly due to the increasing pressures on the resource. Global changes including loss of biodiversity, ecosystems degradation, land use changes, urbanisation, migration and last but most importantly, population growth provoke an ever increasing pressure on water.

Challenges facing the water management sector include potential for socioeconomic and political disturbances; poverty and socioeconomic underdevelopment; lack of information; inequalities in water allocation, knowledge, and military force; geographic advantages; the relative weakness of globally ratified laws and conventions, and especially the weakness of enforcement mechanisms. The water sector also suffers from weak institutions (including lack of democracy and good governance, lack of political will, relative lack of trained human capacity, and lack of financing and other support for the development of institutions).

In short, renewable water resources are extremely sensitive to human activity. And developments concerning water-related questions are therefore inextricably linked to complex socioeconomic factors at every level: local, national and international. Water comes at the crossroads between economic, ecological, social, cultural and even religious issues. The interactions between and among these different areas need to be better understood if we are to have the proper scientific bases for action.

The Pressure on the Resource

The pressure applied by global changes on the resource induces more and more competition, and more competition means higher potential for conflicts.

Adding another level of complications and while organising themselves in an international society, humans have created political borders. They have created, 276 international river basins and 273 international aquifers (counted so far), and as many opportunities for cooperation and competition among various parties with diverging interests, over a vital and shared resource.

One of the critical aims of water management is to continually reconcile such competing interests of water users; be they States sharing a basin or an aquifer, individuals, corporations, interest groups, or administrative entities. The management of water-related conflicts, confrontations, competitions and cooperation is thus a part of water resources management in its broadest sense. This may range from overseeing peaceful cooperation between users of a resource to facilitating negotiation of disputes between sovereign states.

In light of the current global changes and given the important amount of populations living in trans-boundary basins or whose lives depend on water available in trans-boundary aquifers, it is not surprising to count many disputes over the use of freshwater. Conflicts are inherent to human nature. They occur whenever there are differences in interests and objectives between two or more parties on a subject of common interest. However, history has shown that when it comes to water and because of its vital nature, even though conflicts do occur, cooperation happens more often. Furthermore there are more issues about which parties can cooperate over water then issues about which parties can have a conflict. Another interesting lesson from the past is that no war (international armed conflict) has taken place between two or more nations over water in the past 60 years.

The Light at the End of the Tunnel

Humans have always adapted in the long term to a crisis situation. Now the scale of challenges faced is an order of magnitude greater than any known in the past. In order to address the water challenges of the future, we need to preserve, develop and refer to our senses of human solidarity, compassion and ethical standards. Without this, we are jeopardising the quality of life, or even the survival of future generations.

We need to find ways to examine and foster the potential for shared water resources to become a catalyst for regional peace and development through dialogue, cooperation and participatory management of trans-boundary river basins. This is the only way that would allow us to move beyond the words and hopes, and get into action. Action means understanding the complexities of water challenges, addressing them in a holistic manner and supporting cooperation processes through water and for water.

UNESCO's Response

UNESCO's action in the field of water is motivated by these principles. It promotes through its various water programmes, water cooperation through education and science. It uses research and training as entry points to build confidence, trust and dialogue between users of shared water resources. It puts water in humans' minds and solicits their ethical reference system to pave the way for sustainable management decisions and solutions.

The organisation launched in 2000 a programme entitled Potential Conflict to Cooperation Potential (PCCP). PCCP's mission responds to the mandate of UNESCO to construct the defences of peace in the minds of men. It strives to put water in people's mind while nurturing peace and dialogue at various disciplinary and geographical levels.

PCCP uses research and education as venues for scientific cooperation. Under the umbrella of non-threatening and constructive joint work, it brings together key players involved in the management of trans-boundary waters. It offers them a forum for trust building, dialogue and cooperation enhancement. The aim of its activities is to shift water users away from potential conflicts, towards cooperation potential. Such Track II avenues for water diplomacy lay the foundation for actual political cooperation and negotiations: when the level of trust is mature enough, and if all parties concerned are willing, UNESCO can use its intergovernmental leverage power to bring the dialogue to another level of negotiations. The programme uses informal diplomacy to initiate and support cooperation processes among players concerned with the management of water resources. Its focus is on the development of tools which anticipate, prevent and resolve water conflicts.

In order to meet the sustainability requirements of the United Nations' Millennium Development Goals (MDGs), Africa needs an estimated 300 per cent increase in the number of trained water professionals, while Asia needs a 200 per cent increase, and Latin America and the Caribbean a 50 per cent increase. PCCP is helping to develop this needed capacity through global and regional courses. The programme designs and organises training sessions on conflict anticipation, prevention and mitigation in the management of trans-boundary water resources.

Since its inception, PCCP has developed general training material as well as material adapted to the regional specificities of Africa, Latin America, Asia, Europe and the Middle East. In each case, trainers from across the selected regions are involved in the development and delivery of the course material. The trainers come from a variety of fields to ensure the interdisciplinary nature of the course. Once the pilot phase of the training is complete, the course material is evaluated, improved and finalised. It is then made available to local training institutions for further dissemination.

PCCP also organises specialised training sessions for target audiences such as high-level professionals, diplomats and journalists to enhance their negotiation skills, as well as their understanding of trans-boundary water issues. When requested by universities, PCCP incorporates additional topics, such as peaceful management of water resources and alternative dispute resolution (ADR) techniques, into regular post-graduate curricula on water management or peace education.

An 18-month graduate programme was launched under the umbrella of PCCP in 2009 by UNESCO IHE Institute for Water Education in Delft, The Netherlands. It familiarises students with scientific, legal and institutional aspects of water management; it also gives them a range of methods, techniques and tools to apply the acquired knowledge, allows them to critically assess the different functions of existing water resources systems, and enhances their ability to design comprehensive water resources policies and strategies. Two three-week modules on water conflict management which constitute the core part of the programme can be taken as short courses by participants not enrolled in the degree programmes.

The programme has also produced an unprecedented series of publications and online databases that support water management professionals, researchers and students in engineering, economics, geography, geology, and political science in their work on trans-boundary water management. PCCP therefore collaborates with experts from around the world in developing disciplinary studies. By means of extensive research, these studies analyse historical experiences and review existing legal, diplomatic and systems analysis tools, particularly with regard to their utility in resolving water-related conflicts.

In its current research activities on particular cases, PCCP supports cooperative processes related to the management of trans-boundary waters. The case studies' works not only increase knowledge surrounding a selected water body, but promote cooperation among the riparian states concerned with the water resources in question. This is achieved by involving high-level players, governmental advisers, experts and stakeholders who participate in preparing a consensus document reflecting the status of conflict and cooperation in the trans-boundary water body.

The case study process provides a forum to discuss sensitive issues related to the trans-boundary water body, in addition to supporting cooperation, exchange of data and information, and development of the shared resource. Lastly, the process offers stakeholders an opportunity to build a shared vision for the future management of their water resources.

Through its neutral and constructive interventions PCCP supports stakeholders in facing the challenges of managing waters across borders.

Lake Titicaca Case Study

Located in the south of Peru and north-west of Bolivia, the Lake Titicaca Basin is spread over an area of 56,270 km^2. Decades of cooperation led to the creation of the Binational Autonomous Authority of Lake Titicaca (ALT) in 1992. The Ministries of Foreign Affairs of Peru and Bolivia selected experts to write the Lake Titicaca case study and the lessons learned from the joint management of the basin resources were then disseminated through the PCCP programme.

Although much can still be improved in the management of the basin, the PCCP research on the Lake Titicaca helped to avert unilateral decision-making, which could have generated conflicts between the two riparian countries.

Water Diplomacy

Track II mechanisms are indeed well received by water users. They build the cooperation route one block at the time. And they allow decision-makers to engage in political dialogue based on trust and mutual understanding. This sort of diplomacy is especially useful in situations that can be interpreted in a number of different ways, which is usually the case with potential conflicts over shared water resources. Water diplomacy and Track II initiatives are useful when all parties in a relationship recognise that there is a divergence of views while neither side wants the situation spiralling out of control on a vital matter such as water resources. It is indeed economically, environmentally and politically irrational to escalate a situation on water issues.

Water diplomacy is not a theoretical concept nor is it a new idea. It refers to all positive interactions around the management of water resources aiming at achieving peace among, and development of, actors concerned with the uses of such resources. Water diplomacy may involve in its broadest interpretation all kinds and levels of stakeholders, from governments to the civil society. At the international level, States are the main actors of the water diplomacy.

Conclusion

We look at the many emerging trends in today's world in a negative way. But they also bring opportunities. For example, unregulated free markets can hurt poor countries and poor people if they are driven by the sole interest of corporate profits; or they can ensure that those living in poor water-scarce countries have access to food they can afford by ensuring that they have access to markets where they can sell the goods they can produce to earn the needed foreign exchange to buy the food. Other trends that similarly have two sides to them are international relations in the post-cold war era, changing technologies, societal changes (social and economic order), transcultural and transnational civil society, climate change, and environmental and human crises (floods, droughts). The migration of production sites to lower-cost economies can also provide opportunities for developing countries, but must be properly managed to prevent negative side effects. The optimal benefits of all of these opportunities will only occur in a world of peace and trust.

History and a review of experience in the past century both demonstrate that it is possible to manage the scarce resource that is water so that all benefit in a just and equitable manner. There are still many challenges ahead that emerge from changing global physical systems and evolving socioeconomic and political systems. However, as seen above, the PCCP programme has identified a number of tools and mechanisms that will build the capacity and resilience needed to cope with these challenges. There is every reason to hope that the next generation will live in a world with water peace.

RICH
POOR
ECOSYSTEMS
Rustam

HYDRO ETHICS
HYDRO PHILOSOPHY
HYDRO CALLOUSNESS
HYDRO INTELLIGENCE
HYDRO COMMON SENSE
HYDRO RIGHTS
HYDRO POLITICS
HYDRO SOCIOLOGY
HYDRO COMPETITION
HYDRO SOLIDARITY
HYDRO DIPLOMACY
HYDRO PERSUASION
HYDRO LOGIC

SHARING WATER
ACROSS BORDERS

Building Blocks for Good Governance

Herman Havekes

Introduction

In many documents the present water crisis, in which almost half of the global population has no or insufficient access to clean water and sanitary facilities, is called a governance crisis. It is thus very important to examine the concept of good governance.

Naturally, also the more general basic principles of good governance hold, just like in business (corporate governance). A few years ago G.H. Addink has been appointed at Utrecht University as extraordinary professor in administrative legal aspects of good governance. Addink studies the developments of individual principles of good governance (decency, transparency, participation, effectiveness, responsibility and protection of human rights), the implementation of these principles in public administration both in assigning and carrying out administrative tasks, and upholding the principles not only by administration and judge, but also by the National Ombudsman and the Audit Office.

In this paper these general basic principles are left aside and the basic principles for good water governance are at the centre stage. A number of the basic principles of Addink clearly appear to hold for water management as well. In almost the same words these are presented in a White Paper of the EU (openness, participation, accountability, effectiveness and coherence).

The institutional setting of water management in a country is extremely important since it determines effectiveness of water management to a high degree. Are the goals of water management clear? Is it clear what measures have to be carried out to reach these goals? Do these measures connect to policy on different fields, especially spatial planning? Are the goals being reached? Is it clear what public or private organisations are responsible for this? Do organisations act honestly? Is enough money available for the necessary measures? Are legal arrangements with respect to water in place? Are these complied with? Are stakeholders, such as citizens, farmers, fishermen, companies and environmental activists, adequately involved in water management? These kind of institutional questions have to be posed and answered. Together they determine a country's water governance; that may be good or bad depending on the answers to these questions.

Building Blocks

Based on the above-mentioned questions the building blocks of good water governance can be defined. Bucknall (2006) of the World Bank previously made the following discrimination: "Good water governance depends on a number of factors, including strong policy, legal, and regulatory frameworks; more effective implementing organizations; a civic determination to improve water governance; and appropriate investments". The above-mentioned questions result in five building blocks that closely resemble this discrimination by Bucknall:

a) A powerful administrative organisation of water management.
b) A legally embedded system of water law.
c) An adequate financing system and economic analyses of water measures.
d) A systematic approach.
e) The participation of stakeholders.

These building blocks can be outlined as follows. This is not an exhaustive overview.

Administrative Organisation

A powerful and clear administrative organisation is needed for an effective implementation of water management. The water responsibilities and jurisdictions of the organisations involved must be absolutely clear. Within this framework water responsibilities refer to water safety, the management of surface and groundwater quantity and quality, fresh water supply, sewage and waste water treatment. In other words: water system and water chain. Abroad irrigation is often one of the most important responsibilities. Choices may differ, e.g., more government and less market, or less government and more market, centralised or decentralised, general administration or functional water organisations; as long as it is absolutely clear who is responsible. Besides, internationally there is a trend of organisations based on catchments (River Basin Approach). Also some kind of decentralisation can be observed in which jurisdictions are assigned to local interest groups of farmers and fishermen. The Dutch water boards certainly are not the only example of this, as some people may think. Many organisations have regional water authorities, be it different from our water boards. This development reminds of the philosophy of the Common Pool Resource Management of Nobel Price winner Elinor Ostrom. In Europe a decentralised approach matches the principle of subsidiarity. In this respect, the decentralised capacity in water management, including professionalism, knowledge, skills to collaborate, and willingness to participate, is an important boundary condition for a successful decentraliszation.

It is important that different government bodies coordinate their tasks and collaborate assuming a certain administrative organisation of water management in a country that usually is not easy to change. Coherence between different administrative layers that have responsibilities in water management is essential. There must also be coherence between different administrative sectors (water, spatial planning, environment, nature, economic development, energy supply, agriculture, shipping, etc.). In our own country this coordination is even statutory for waste water treatment, in which communities manage the sewage system and the water boards the waste water treatment plants (article 3.8 of the Water Act). Improved coordination in waste water treatment should result in € 380 million costs reduction annually, according to an administrative agreement on water issues (Bestuursakkoord Water).

From an administrative, official and financial perspective, the administrative organisation of water management must be sufficiently powerful to address the many challenges effectively and efficiently. The government will especially need sufficient information, sufficient data to substantiate water policy. This information will have to be made available to stakeholders as well.

A lot is thus expected from authorities that have responsibilities on water issues. Are the right things being done, and in the right way? Authorities especially will need the essential multidisciplinary knowledge and will have to be open to innovations. Only then can water management take its place in the coordination with management of the physical environment in a broader sense, especially with spatial planning. In many countries and on many places (deltas) insufficient coordination between water management and spatial planning, in which spatial planning usually dominates, is a major problem. Too much fragmentation of responsibilities over many organisations, such as in Flanders, therefore should be avoided. The division of responsibilities then becomes transparent to outsiders. Stakeholders in water management know who to turn to when needed. A situation like with the Xintia disaster in France in early 2010, when it was not clear who was responsible for the broken dikes, should be avoided. Wherever in the world the government (inevitably) plays an important role in water management (see article 21 of our Constitution and the fact that even fresh water supply is globally controlled by public bodies for 85%), it is only fair to demand from the government to do so in a just and transparent way. Globally corruption is often a bottleneck in water management. The Water Integrity Network in Berlin aims to fight corruption in water management. That is exactly why it is important for the government to be transparent and to be accountable for its actions. Thus, the government can get the stakeholders to support measures that need to be taken. Trust, therefore, is essential for reaching water goals.

Water Law

In water management the appraisal between the general and the individual interest always plays a role. What is beneficial to many can be detrimental to an individual landowner or company, and vice versa. If anyone can do whatever he wants (drain, extract, fill up, build etc.) water management will lead to nowhere. Sometimes no has to be the answer and certain activities have to be regulated through permits or even forbidden. The all-out effort must be expropriation (for building civil-engineering works such as dams, dikes and waterways). It must be possible for the general interest to overrule the individual one, the right for individual compensation of damage remaining in full force. In some countries where property rights play an important role or where long-lasting water concessions have been given (Spain, Switzerland) it is difficult to give precedence to general interests over individual property rights. Still the government will need such jurisdictions and these should be statutory in a constitutional state. Also generally a number of starting points for water management must be statutory. Elements that must be part of an adequate system of water law are certain prohibitions, commands, tolerance obligations, arrangements for compensating damage, a systematic approach, a financing system, jurisdictions for normal and calamitous circumstances, enforcement, sanctions, and a system of participation and protection of rights. Anyway, each country makes its own choices, depending on circumstances, culture and the legal system. In a number of countries for instance, also in Europe, the entitlement to water is statutory, while in The Netherlands, where everyone has access to drinking water, this is not the case. This international diversity is not a problem and is unavoidable to a certain level; there has to be an orderly and coherent water legislation to be able to stimulate and guarantee the water law to function adequately. Fragmentation into numerous acts and implementing regulations must be avoided.

International coordination and settling disputes on water also ask for regulations because water issues are often cross-boundary. Partly these regulations have been laid down in writing in international treaties, such as the Helsinki Treaty on cross-boundary waters. This also holds for treaties between two or more countries on the distribution of water of cross-boundary rivers. Specifically for Europe 15 EC directives have been laid down in writing, of which the Water Framework Directive and the Flood Risk Directive are the most familiar. EU member states have to follow these directives. Water law thus has both a national and international character.

Enforcement of, and compliance with regulations is at least as important as having a statutory water law system. For this the government needs to have instruments for sanctions. A wonderful water regulation may quite easily be organised, it loses its function, however, when enforcement and compliance are not in place. Egypt probably has the most advanced water quality regulation in the world, but it is not enforced and therefore it does not work. In a number of countries the lack of adequate regulation is not the problem, but the fact that citizens, farmers and companies hardly comply with it is (e.g., Bangladesh, Colombia, Yemen). In view of compliance it is naturally essential that the regulation matches the culture and the legal system of the country in question; the logic and reasonability of it need to be clear to the society and the society needs to have confidence that the legislation serves its interests. It may be wise to pay attention to administrative legal instruments to enforce the law since the criminal enforcement abroad does not always function optimally.

Adequate Financing System and Economic Analyses of Water Measures

This building block has both a receipts and expenditure side. There must be enough receipts to finance water management. Investments are sound when those receipts are spent as efficiently and effectively as possible. A lot of money is involved in water management. Investments have to be made in dikes, pumps, sluices, irrigation systems, water treatment plants, drinking water supply, and the sewage system. All of these will have to be maintained on a regular basis, and will have to be renewed in due time. The same holds for the water systems; good management and maintenance are needed, for instance by dredging every now and then. If this is not done regularly, big problems arise (reduction discharge capacity, floods). In developing countries, the situation is often the same. Discharge canals get blocked because of the waste people dump. Money is therefore needed, not only for capital-intensive investments, but for daily management and maintenance as well. This costs a lot of money. A relatively small country such as The Netherlands at the moment spends some € 6.5 billion in water management annually, which is about € 400 per citizen. It is essential that this money is available indeed, in order to avoid problems and to fix and maintain water management. The (central) government can take care of this and finance water management from general means. Experience has shown, however, that the central government is responsible for a great number of tasks that all cost money (education, civil defence, health care, transportation). Because of this, not enough money is made available for water management on a regular basis. The fact that water management often asks for investments and measures on the long run, thus making them seem less spectacular and urgent, adds to this. As far as our own country is concerned: it is statutory that the central governments pays 100 per cent of the costs for strengthening the primary flood defences (see article 7.23 of the Water Act) but not all of the money that is needed can be made available on the national budget. Because of this, part of the costs has been laid down at the water boards through a so-called emergency act. Other countries often have the same financial problems.

In this respect the philosophy of the European Water Framework Directive is interesting. Article 9 in this Directive anticipates reclaiming the costs of water services including, also in international law accepted, the principle that the polluter has to pay. Water services are: drinking water supply, the sewage system, and water treatment. The Water Framework Directive states these tasks should no longer (completely) be financed through general means, but (also) by stakeholders including at least households, agriculture and companies. This way stakeholders more or less pay for the costs of water management themselves. Dutch water management already is largely based on this principle; the central government covers only some 15 per cent of the total costs of water management. The major part of the costs is charged to the consumers by water companies, communities, and water boards through pricing and taxes. The receipts are assured of and labelled at the same time: the money can only be used for water management. In other countries, however, the principle of reclaiming costs is hardly in place: drinking water, for instance, often is for free. The European approach seems to be an interesting option to adequately finance water management. It is a problem though that politicians do not get statues by introducing new taxes and prices; this can be taken into account by starting at a relative low price level.

Naturally, the receipts will have to be used as efficiently and effectively as possible, by spending them on the right issues. Using integral economic analyses, as mentioned in article 5 of the Water Framework Directive, is vital at this. In many countries water is scarce and needs to be divided over several purposes based on conscious decisions. Economic considerations may play a role at this. Will the sewage systems be dimensioned to drain heavy downpour that occurs once every 100 years, against high costs, or do we accept flooding of the streets every now and then, and compensate damage? Do we take all possible measures to prevent a flood from happening or do we invest more energy and money in flood warning systems, evacuation procedures or emergency measures (England)? Is desalination of seawater cost-effective for certain cultures or not? These are only a few questions that economic analyses can answer. Insofar these are part of adequately financing water management.

Systematic Approach

In the foregoing it is mentioned that water management is about taking a wide range of measures on the long run. A long time ahead measures will have to be defined and implemented to be prepared for developments in the (far) future (climate change, sea level rise, salt intrusion, soil subsidence, urbanisation, etc.). A highly systematic approach is needed for this. This way, goals in water management can be defined, the essential measures can be developed, their mutual relations can be assessed and compared with, and tuned to developments on many other fields, such as spatial planning, nature and environmental management, agriculture and horticulture, transportation, energy supply, urbanisation and economic development. Balancing and awarding functions needs to be an important part of the systematic approach; competing functions will thus emerge, and solid and conscious choices can be made. In this respect integral plans are preferred, in which all water interests are considered. Many countries are becoming more aware of the importance of this, and the slogan is integrated water resources management (IWRM).

Also, internationally, tuning water management to spatial planning is especially crucial. In many (delta) countries people compete for the same piece of land while it is sometimes more wise to use that land for water purposes. If it is not used for water, the water will take the land anyway resulting in disastrous consequences. A systematic approach can contribute that water gets its space in time in all spatial developments and a fait accompli can be avoided. The water assessment of Flanders and The Netherlands is especially linked to spatial plans from other regional and local authorities (provinces and communities). A systematic approach helps to determine the amount of money that is needed for the measures; thus (costly) ad hoc measures can be avoided that appear less successful in the long run. A systematic approach is also the instrument to get the stakeholders closely involved in water policy and water management in time. Thanks to early involvement an optimal connection can be made to the preferences in society, even though choices sometimes cannot be avoided and not all preferences can be met. A systematic approach also offers good opportunities to discuss cross-boundary water issues with neighbour countries. Interests upstream and downstream will have to be discussed at the same level in order to avoid conflicts. A large number of steps still have to be taken internationally in this respect. Unfortunately water use too often is still the cause of international disputes. Ideally joint plans are made in these cross-boundary situations. At least there should be coordination in the beginning of these plans.

Experience with this systematic approach in The Netherlands goes back almost 50 years. Our planning system may be somewhat over the top though, and it will be cleared thoroughly through the administrative agreement on water issues (Bestuursakkoord Water); the principle and the value of this approach are not under debate, however. European water policy is also characterised by a strong systematic approach, especially the obliged catchment management plans and the flood risk management plans from the Water Framework Directive and the Flood Risk Directive. The awareness that this systematic approach is necessary is growing in other countries (Indonesia) and delta plans are being prepared (Viet Nam).

Participation of Stakeholders

The government does not exist for its own purposes, but has to serve society. Governmental policy has to be aimed at fulfilling just societal wishes where possible and achievable. This holds for government tasks in general and for water management in particular. Water, after all, is a public resource and belongs to all of us. Many stakeholder groups are involved in water management: households, farmers, fishermen, companies, conservationists and environmentalists, shipmasters, vacationers, etc. They all have specific wishes with respect to water management that are not infrequently in conflict. Agriculture, for instance, benefits from groundwater levels that are not too high while nature interests generally ask for higher water levels. Companies would like to settle and do business wherever they please while vacationers want to enjoy water without being disturbed. In this respect choices have to be made. Interests have to be balanced, which is the primacy of the government. Water management gains strength if all those different interests are served as much as possible, and if choices that cannot be avoided are discussed and explained. This holds especially for numerous measures where the collaboration of certain stakeholders is simply needed. Agriculture, for instance, where farmers often own the land where measures have to be taken. Also, one has to realise that these stakeholders often have to pay for the measures through pricing and taxes; good participation is needed for more than one reason.

In this respect the Dutch water boards are interesting because the important stakeholders (citizens, farmers, companies and nature managers) are represented directly in the administration of the water board. Their participation is institutionalised that way. In many other countries that have separate water organisations, a development in this direction can be observed, and representatives of interest groups take part in the administration of regional and local water users organisations. Besides this administrative representation there has to be a participative and interactive approach in which all interest groups can express their views and can come up with unsolicited ideas. More generally, this involvement asks for good procedures for making important decisions (dike reinforcement projects, building dams and irrigation systems, making wells, sewage systems and treatment plants, licensing, water level agreements, prohibitions to extract water, etc.). These procedures have to give room to all stakeholders to present their views on measures. Ideally, they should be convinced that they are heard and they should have faith in the authorities. If their views cannot be met, they must have the possibility to bring the decision before the judge. This is laid down for Europe in the Aarhus Treaty. Some countries even have special 'water judges' (South Africa, and in Spain El Tribunal de las Aguas de Vega de Valencia that already exists over 1000 years). More specifically the above-mentioned systematic approach can also be extremely useful for these countries. A timely and intensive discussion of the design of these plans with all those involved can strengthen the understanding and the support for their implementation. For good reason the Water Framework Directive states that the design of the catchment management plan has to be available for inspection for one year.

Final Remark

In this paper five building blocks for good water governance have been discriminated and shortly clarified. Successively these are a powerful administrative organisation of water management, a legally embedded system of water law, an adequate financing system and economic analyses of water measures, a systematic approach, and the participation of stakeholders. Together these building blocks determine the strength of water governance. Obviously, these building blocks can be elaborated more or less, and in different ways, in different countries. Clearly, without these building blocks there is no good water governance though. Insofar they can be useful in the assessment of water governance all over the world.

✧

ECOSYSTEMS FOR LIFE

A Bangladesh-India Initiative

Bangladesh and India have some of the most intricate and complex river systems in the world. The Ganges, Brahmaputra and Meghna, the three major rivers, along with their tributaries drain an area of about 1.75 million square kilometres and have direct impact on around 620 million people. These great rivers are inseparable from the history and legends of the region, as well to the people who depend on them for their well-being. Strategies to ensure the future well-being of the region are needed.

Ecosystems for Life: A Bangladesh-India Initiative, is an IUCN lead multi-stakeholder dialogue process to promote better management of natural resources in Bangladesh and India. The initiative works to develop a shared vision and understanding of food, livelihood and water security issues through collaborative research and studies, creation of a knowledge hub, developing research-based policy options and enhancing the capacity of civil society stakeholders to participate in the management of natural resources.

To address food, livelihood and water security issues, Ecosystems for Life focuses on four main areas of research. It explores the links between food security and water productivity for poverty alleviation. It conducts research on the impacts of climate change, adaptation methods and mitigating strategies. It studies the costs and benefits of using river based transportation as opposed to other cross-country transportation systems. Finally, it examines the links between economic development and environmental security.

Ecosystems for Life is being implemented in Bangladesh and India by IUCN Country Offices and managed by the IUCN Asia Regional Office, Bangkok, Thailand. The four and a half year initiative is supported by the Embassy of the Kingdom of the Netherlands.

Learn more at: *www.iucn.org/E4L*

BRIDGE: Building River Dialogue and Governance

BRIDGE is an IUCN project aimed at building water governance capacities, through learning, demonstration, leadership, and consensus-building, in particular in transboundary river basins.

Water governance sets the 'rules of the game' for the way water is managed. It determines how, or even whether, sustainable water resource management is implemented. Poor water governance results in degradation and over-allocation of water resources, is a cause of vulnerability for poor people, and leads to weaker and less resilient livelihoods and economic growth.

Policies, laws, and institutions are the three pillars of water governance within a country, as well as in a transboundary basin, where they are complemented by the agreements negotiated between basin countries. In order for this governance to be effective, countries need to develop their own water governance capacity (WGC) through transparent, coherent, and cost-efficient policies, laws, and institutions.

BRIDGE is implemented in 9 transboundary river basins worldwide:

- *South America:* Zarumilla river (Ecuador-Peru), Catamayo-Chira river (Ecuador-Peru), Lake Titicaca basin (Peru-Bolivia)
- *Mesoamerica:* Coatan river (Mexico-Guatemala), Goascoran river (Honduras-El Salvador), Sixaola river (Costa Rica-Panama)
- *Mekong region:* Sekong (Vietnam-Lao PDRCambodia), Sre Pok (Vietnam-Cambodia), Sesan river (Vietnam-Cambodia)

The Sekong, Sesan and Sre Pok rivers of Cambodia, Lao PDR and Vietnam are the only trans-boundary tributaries of the Mekong. The 3S rivers – as they are collectively called – are instrumental in the hydrology of the Lower Mekong, contributing up to 18 percent of its annual total discharge.

The 3S river basin is also a breadbasket for the livelihoods of over 3 million people, many of whom depend directly on the rivers' resources. As the Asian region develops, and considering the basin's high irrigation and hydropower potential, the 3S rivers are expected to continue playing a significant role in the economic growth of the basin, and the region as a whole.

Collaborative trans-boundary governance is central to the sustainable and efficient use of water management resources in the 3S river basin. IUCN, under the umbrella of the Building River Dialogue and Governance (BRIDGE) project supported by the Swiss Agency for Development and Cooperation (SDC), seeks to facilitate cooperative processes in the 3S region, by developing and strengthening water governance capacities through governance reforms, stakeholder dialogues and knowledge exchange programmes.

Learn more at: *www.iucn.org/asia_water, www.3sbasin.org*